A Midsummer Night's Dream

SHAKESPEARE IN PERFORMANCE

Advisory Editors: **David Bevington and Peter Holland**

methuen | dra...

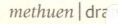

30131 04433271 3

CHECK FOR
C.D AT
BACK OF BOOK!

First UK edition published 2007

A & C Black Publishers Limited
38 Soho Square
London W1D 3HB
www.acblack.com

© 2006 Sourcebooks Inc.
First printed in the U.S. by Sourcebooks MediaFusion

ISBN 978-0-7136-8358-5

A CIP catalogue record for this book is available from the British Library.

This book is produced using paper that is made from wood grown in managed, sustainable forests. It is natural, renewable and recyclable. The logging and manufacturing processes conform to the environmental regulations of the country of origin.

Cover Design by Jocelyn Lucas

Cover Illustration © Ann Elson 2007

CD manufactured by Lemon Media

Printed and bound in Great Britain by The Bath Press, Bath

To students, teachers, and lovers of Shakespeare

Contents

About Sourcebooks MediaFusion

Launched with the 1998 *New York Times* bestseller
We Interrupt This Broadcast and formally founded in 2000,
Sourcebooks MediaFusion is the nation's leading publisher
of mixed-media books. This revolutionary imprint is dedicated
to creating original content—be it audio, video, CD-ROM,
or Web—that is fully integrated with the books we create.
The result, we hope, is a new, richer, eye-opening,
thrilling experience with books for our readers.
Our experiential books have become both bestsellers
and classics in their subjects, including poetry (*Poetry Speaks*),
children's books (*Poetry Speaks to Children*),
history (*We Shall Overcome*), sports (*And The Crowd Goes Wild*),
the plays of William Shakespeare, and more.
See what's new from us at www.sourcebooks.com.

About the Text

The earliest edition of *A Midsummer Night's Dream* was printed in 1600
in quarto form, and that serves as the copy-text for this edition.
The punctuation and the spelling of the quarto has been silently
modernized in this text, although significant variations are recorded
in the notes and speech prefixes have been regularized,
usually without notation.

On the CD

1. Introduction to the Sourcebooks Shakespeare
   A Midsummer Night's Dream by Derek Jacobi

ACT 1, SCENE 1, LINES 20–64

2. Narration by Derek Jacobi
3. Paul Shelley as Theseus, Amanda Root as Hermia
   Arkangel Shakespeare • 2003
4. David Timson as Egeus, Jack Ellis as Theseus, Cathy Sara as Hermia
   Naxos • 1997

ACT 1, SCENE 1, LINES 177–203

5. Narration by Derek Jacobi
6. Saskia Wickham as Helena, Amanda Root as Hermia
   Arkangel Shakespeare • 2003
7. Emily Raymond as Helena, Cathy Sara as Hermia
   Naxos • 1997

ACT 1, SCENE 2, LINES 9–53

8. Narration by Derek Jacobi
9. Richard Cordery as Quince, Roy Hudd as Bottom, Alex Lowe as
   Flute, Sidney Livingstone as Starveling, John Hollis as Snout
   Arkangel Shakespeare • 2003
10. John Moffatt as Quince, Warren Mitchell as Bottom, Peter Kenny as
    Flute, John Rye as Starveling, Don McCorkindale as Snout
    Naxos • 1997

ACT 2, SCENE 1, LINES 60–87

11. Narration by Derek Jacobi
12. David Harewood as Oberon, Adjoa Andoh as Titania
    Arkangel Shakespeare • 2003
13. Michael Maloney as Oberon, Sarah Woodward as Titania
    Naxos • 1997

ACT 2, SCENE 1, LINES 249–267

14. Narration by Derek Jacobi
15. Sir John Gielgud as Oberon
16. Michael Maloney as Oberon
    Naxos • 1997

ACT 2, SCENE 2, LINES 72–89

17. Narration by Derek Jacobi
18. Richard McCabe as Puck
    Arkangel Shakespeare • 2003
19. Ian Hughes as Puck
    Naxos • 1997

ACT 3, SCENE 1, LINES 63–84

20. Narration by Derek Jacobi
21. Roy Hudd as Bottom, Richard Cordery as Quince,
    Richard McCabe as Puck, Alex Lowe as Flute
    Arkangel Shakespeare • 2003
22. Warren Mitchell as Bottom, John Moffatt as Quince,
    Ian Hughes as Puck, Peter Kenny as Flute
    Naxos • 1997

ACT 3, SCENE 1, LINES 95–132

23. Narration by Derek Jacobi
24. Roy Hudd as Bottom, Adjoa Andoh as Titania
    Arkangel Shakespeare • 2003
25. Warren Mitchell as Bottom, Sarah Woodward as Titania
    Naxos • 1997

ACT 3, SCENE 2, LINES 7–35

26. Narration by Derek Jacobi
27. Sir John Gielgud as Puck
28. Ian Hughes as Puck
    Naxos • 1997

Act 3, Scene 2, Lines 301–346

29. Narration by Derek Jacobi
30. Saskia Wickham as Helena, Amanda Root as Hermia,
    Rupert Penry-Jones as Lysander, Clarence Smith as Demetrius
    Arkangel Shakespeare • 2003
31. Emily Raymond as Helena, Cathy Sara as Hermia,
    Benjamin Soames as Lysander, Jamie Glover as Demetrius
    Naxos • 1997

Act 3, Scene 2, Lines 356–379

32. Narration by Derek Jacobi
33. Sir John Gielgud as Oberon
34. Michael Maloney as Oberon
    Naxos • 1997

Act 4, Scene 1, Lines 42–80

35. Narration by Derek Jacobi
36. David Harewood as Oberon, Adjoa Andoh as Titania,
    Richard McCabe as Puck
    Arkangel Shakespeare • 2003
37. Michael Maloney as Oberon, Sarah Woodward as Titania,
    Ian Hughes as Puck
    Naxos • 1997

Act 4, Scene 1, Lines 141–188

38. Narration by Derek Jacobi
39. Rupert Penry-Jones as Lysander, Clarence Smith as Demetrius,
    Paul Shelley as Theseus, Amanda Root as Hermia,
    Saskia Wickham as Helena
    Arkangel Shakespeare • 2003
40. Benjamin Soames as Lysander, David Timson as Egeus,
    Jamie Glover as Demetrius, Jack Ellis as Theseus, Cathy Sara as Her-
    mia, Emily Raymond as Helena
    Naxos • 1997

Featured Audio Productions

LIVING SHAKESPEARE (1962)

Theseus	Tenniel Evans
Hippolyta	Agnes Bernelle
Egeus	Carl Bernard
Hermia	Ingrid Hafner
Demetrius	Peter Birrel
Lysander	Richard Gale
Helena	Sarah Churchill
Quince	Bill Horsley
Bottom	Stanley Holloway
Flute	Julian Holloway
Starveling	Carl Bernard
Snout	Alastair Hunter
Snug	Gerald Lawson
Fairy	Agnes Bernelle
Oberon	Kenneth Griffith
Titania	Adrienne Corri
Puck	Annette Crosbie
Philostrate	Carl Bernard
Narrator	Dennis Vance

THE COMPLETE ARKANGEL SHAKESPEARE (2003)

Bottom	Roy Hudd
Hermia	Amanda Root
Helena	Saskia Wickham
Lysander	Rupert Penry-Jones
Demetrius	Clarence Smith
Puck	Richard McCabe
Oberon	David Harewood
Titania	Adjoa Andoh
Quince	Richard Cordery
Snout	John Hollis
Flute	Alex Lowe
Starveling	Sidney Livingstone
Snug	John Dallimore
Theseus	Paul Shelley
Hippolyta	Sophie Heyman
Fairy	Aicha Kossoko

NAXOS AUDIOBOOKS (1997)

Theseus	Jack Ellis
Hippolyta	Karen Archer
Lysander	Benjamin Soames
Demetrius	Jamie Glover
Hermia	Cathy Sara
Helena	Emily Raymond
Oberon	Michael Maloney
Titania	Sarah Woodward
Puck	Ian Hughes
Quince	John Moffatt
Bottom	Warren Mitchell
Flute	Peter Kenny
Snout	Don McCorkindale
Snug/Egeus	David Timson
Starveling/Philostrate	John Rye

SELECTED SPEECHES BY SIR JOHN GIELGUD

Note from the Series Editors

For many of us, our first and only encounter with Shakespeare was in school. We may recall that experience as a struggle, working through dense texts filled with unfamiliar words. However, those of us who were fortunate enough to have seen a play performed have altogether different memories. It may be of an interesting scene or an unusual character, but it is most likely a speech. Often, just hearing part of one instantly transports us to that time and place. "Friends, Romans, countrymen, lend me your ears," "But, soft! What light through yonder window breaks?," "To sleep, perchance to dream," "Tomorrow, and tomorrow, and tomorrow."

The Sourcebooks Shakespeare series is our attempt to use the power of performance to help you experience the play. In the series, you will see photographs from various productions, on film and on stage, historical and contemporary, known worldwide or in your community. You may recognize some actors you didn't know were Shakespearean performers. You can explore set drawings, costume designs, and scene edits, all reproduced from original notes. Finally, on the enclosed audio CD, listen to scenes from the play as performed by some of the most accomplished Shakespeareans of our times. Often, we include multiple interpretations of the same scene, showing you the remarkable richness of the text. Hear the great Sir John Gielgud in a recording from the 1930s reciting a speech of Puck's. Compare that to a contemporary version made in 2003. The actors create different characters, different meanings, different worlds.

As you read the text of the play, you can consult explanatory notes for definitions of unfamiliar words and phrases or words whose meanings have changed. These notes appear on the left pages, next to the text of the play. The audio, photographs, and other production artifacts augment the notes and they too are indexed to the appropriate lines. Use the pictures to see how others have staged a particular scene and get ideas on costumes, scenery, blocking, etc. As for the audio, each track represents a particular interpretation of a scene. Sometimes, a passage that's difficult to comprehend opens up when you hear it out loud. Furthermore, when you hear more than one version, you gain a keener understanding of the characters. Did Egeus mean it? Will he have his daughter put to death should she refuse to marry the man to whom she is promised? The actors made their choices and so can you. You may even come up with your own unique interpretation.

The text of the play, the definitions, the production notes, the audio—all of these work together, and they are included for your enjoyment. Because the audio is excerpts of performances, it is meant to entertain. When you see a passage with an associated clip, you can read along as you hear the actors perform the scenes for you. Or you can sit back, close your eyes, and listen, and then go back and reread the text with a new perspective. Finally, since the text is actually a script, you may find yourself reciting the lines out loud and doing your own performance!

You will undoubtedly notice that some of the audio does not exactly match the text. Also, there are photographs and facsimiles of scenes that aren't in your edition. There are many reasons for this, but foremost among them is the fact that Shakespeare scholarship continues to move forward and the prescribed ways of dealing with and interpreting text is always changing. Thus a play that was edited and published in the 1900s will be different from one published in 2005. It may also surprise you to know that there usually isn't one definitive early edition of a Shakespeare play. *A Midsummer Night's Dream* was first printed in quarto form in 1600. Second Quarto, First Folio, and Second Folio editions followed. Finally, artists have their own interpretation of the play and they too cut and change lines and scenes according to their vision. Productions in the eighteenth century were heavily cut; they primarily focused on either the fairies or the Mechanicals.

The ways in which *A Midsummer Night's Dream* has been presented have varied considerably through the years. We've included essays in the book to give you glimpses into the range of the productions, showing you how other artists have approached the play and providing examples of just what changes were made and how. Professor Peter Holland writes, as a scholar and a fan, of director Peter Brook's seminal Royal Shakespeare Company production from 1970. "In Production," an essay by our text editor, Terri Bourus, provides an overview of how the play has been performed through the years, from its early history where the focus was on the fairies and the Mechanicals through Madame Vestris's naturalistic staging of the entire play in the 1840s to contemporary films and theater productions. In "'That You Have but Slumbered Here': *A Midsummer Night's Dream* in Popular Culture," Douglas Lanier cites myriad examples of pop appropriations from music, children's literature, comics, and cartoons. Ironically, due to its erotic themes, *A Midsummer Night's Dream* also has the dubious distinction of being the Shakespearean play most frequently alluded to in pornographic film titles. Finally, for the actor in you (and for those who want to peek behind the curtain), we have two essays that you may find especially intriguing. Andrew Wade, voice coach of the Royal Shakespeare Company for sixteen years, shares his point of view on how to understand the text and speak it. You can also listen in on him as he works with an actor on the opening speech of the play; perhaps you too can learn the art of speaking Shakespeare. The last essay is from an interview we conducted in which we talked to each member of a cast, asking the actors about their characters and relationships. We found it fascinating to hear what they had to say on various topics: for example, the relationship between Oberon and Titania, or the differences between Helena and Hermia and the contrasting lack of differences between Lysander and Demetrius. The characters come to life in a way that's different from reading the book or watching a performance.

One last note: we are frequently asked why we didn't include the whole play, either in audio or video. While we enjoy the plays and are avid theatergoers, we are trying to do something more with the audio (and the production notes and the essays) than just presenting them to you. In fact, our goal is to provide you tools that will enable you to explore the play on your own, from many different directions. Our hope is that the different pieces of audio, the voices of the actors, and the classic production photos and notes will all engage you and illuminate the play on many levels, so that you can construct your own understanding and create your own "production," a fresh interpretation unique to you.

Though the productions we reference and the audio clips we include are but a miniscule sample of the play's history, we hope they encourage you to further delve into the works of Shakespeare. New editions of the play come out yearly; movie adaptations are regularly being produced; there are hundreds of theater groups in the U.S. alone; and performances could be going on right in your backyard. We echo the words of noted writer and poet Robert Graves, who said, "The remarkable thing about Shakespeare is that he is really very good—in spite of all the people who say he is very good."

We welcome you now to the Sourcebooks Shakespeare edition of *A Midsummer Night's Dream.*

Dominique Raccah and Marie Macaisa
Series Editors

Introduction to the Sourcebooks Shakespeare *A Midsummer Night's Dream*
Derek Jacobi

track 1

In Production:

A Midsummer Night's Dream THROUGH THE YEARS

Terri Bourus

The 1623 Folio of Shakespeare's plays lists fourteen titles under the heading of "Comedies," among them, *A Midsummer Night's Dream*. Previously published in a 1600 quarto format, the title page of that text tells us all we know about the earliest performances of this play: it "hath been sundry times publikely acted, by the right Honorable, the Lord Chamberlaine his servants." There are three early references to the play (1604, 1624, and 1630), plus another in 1631 that mentions the Mechanicals (the workmen) and Robin "goode-fellow." The play was likely written during the winter of 1594 and 1595, possibly for a royal wedding with Elizabeth I herself in attendance. We know it was in the repertoire of Shakespeare's company by 1598.

A rendition of one of the earliest performances in an Elizabethan playhouse
Mary Evans Picture Library

A Midsummer Night's Dream reflects, in many important ways, the England of Shakespeare's day. The audience crowded around the spare stages of London's early theaters would have been familiar with the fairies, hobgoblins, and sprites that were said to populate the forest around "Athens." Robin Goodfellow was a "puck" or hobgoblin that frequented the hearths of English domestic life; in the folklore of the day, he was thought to play tricks on housemaids who did not treat him well. In addition to English folklore, Shakespeare drew on Chaucer's *The Knight's Tale,* Greek and Roman mythology and history, Germanic myth, and even scripture. He brought his sources together and stamped them with his own indelible and unique mark. For example, he took the story of "Pyramus & Thisbe" from Ovid's *Metamorphoses* and, by skillfully drawing out the play through a performance by amateurs, turns tragedy into comedy.

Our knowledge about how its original audience reacted to this play is quite limited. However, with its familiar characters and popular themes, we can imagine this play to have been well received. The audiences may have responded quietly or even rudely to the pompousness of the Court, gaily to the plight of the lovers, and raucously to those rude workmen who stage the play-within-the-play, "Pyramus & Thisbe." It seems plausible that Shakespeare was representing, through the adventures of Quince, Bottom, Flute, Snout, Snug, and Starveling, his own experiences as a Player and a playwright.

THE COMMONWEALTH PERIOD AND THE RESTORATION

After Shakespeare's death in 1616 and the publication of the Folio in 1623, the sociopolitical situation in England changed the culture irrevocably. Viewed by the Puritans as encouraging sinfulness and decadence, the theaters were closed once Cromwell took control of the government in 1642. However, "entertainments" were never completely eliminated and after the Commonwealth dissolved, they once again emerged as an important part of English culture. Even so, there are few references to *The Dream,* as it is known in theatrical circles, after the theaters were reopened in 1660 under Charles II. The play simply may not have seemed adaptable to the high wit of Restoration theater and was rarely, if ever, staged.

A shortened and drastically altered version of the play, *The Merry Conceited Humours of Bottom the Weaver*, appeared in print in 1661. Over thirty years later, in 1692, Henry Purcell staged a ballet version of the play, calling it *The Fairy Queen*. Neither of these adaptations stood the test of time. *Humours* was a droll and rather simplistic entertainment of the Commonwealth, coming to print during the early Restoration period. This version deleted the lovers and most of the lyrical language of the now-depleted fairy band. Lengthy, garish, and ostentatious, Purcell's ballet was simply too expensive to stage. Samuel Pepys recorded seeing a performance of *A Midsummer Night's Dream* on September 26, 1662. He wrote in his diary that the play was "insipid" and "ridiculous" and he vowed to never see it again. There was little chance of that happening in any case—*The Dream* seems not to have been staged again until 1763, and once again, it was a failure, closing after only one performance.

THE ROMANTIC AND VICTORIAN STAGE PRODUCTIONS: *A Midsummer Night's Dream* IN THE EIGHTEENTH AND NINETEENTH CENTURIES

Although seven different adaptations were produced in the eighteenth century, they were heavily cut and altered, with the emphasis placed primarily on either the fairies or the Mechanicals. They include *Pyramus and Thisbe* in 1716 and again in 1745. David Garrick, who was one of the few actors to regularly stage Shakespeare's plays in the eighteenth century, mounted three adaptations: *The Fairies* in 1755, and *The Fairies* and *A Fairy Tale* in 1763. *A Midsummer Night's Dream* would not be staged in its entirety again until 1840, when the noted actress, singer, dancer, and theater manager, Madame Lucia Elizabetta Bartolozzi Vestris (1797–1856) staged the play in Covent Garden, London. What delightful irony that it was a woman who would resurrect a play that, in its original production, could have only been acted by men (witness the hilarity of Flute as Thisbe, interpreted by Joe E. Brown in Reinhardt's 1935 film, with his dress falling off of his masculine shoulders and hairy chest). Madame Vestris rented London's Olympic Theater, becoming the first woman to be a theater manager. She insisted on using real trees for props, introduced the boxed stage to the theater, and eventually came to manage Covent Garden, where she began to stage Shakespeare's plays. In her second season, she produced *A Midsummer Night's Dream* and assumed the role of the fairy king Oberon, complete with tunic and tights. Using

Shakespeare's original script, Madame Vestris cut some of the dialogue but did not alter the text significantly or add anything new. She introduced London to the music of Felix Mendelssohn (1809–1847), which would quickly become the common incidental music for the play. She also included music by Beethoven and Weber, giving new life to Shakespeare's play after nearly two hundred years of failed adaptations and obscurity. Madame Vestris's acclaimed production for the London stage influenced most subsequent stagings of *The Dream* until the mid-twentieth century.

The formidable Madame Lucia Elizabetta Bartolozzi Vestris from an 1837 lithograph
Mary Evans Picture Library

With the success of the Vestris production, *The Dream* became a must-do for most London theater companies and, given the conventions of Victorian theater and the nature of competition, the staging became increasingly elaborate. Samuel Phelps (1804–1878) produced the play at Sadler's Wells in 1853 and Charles Kean (1811–1868), the son of the famous Shakespearean actor Edmund Kean (1789–1833), responded with lavish staging that stressed the Grecian elements of the play. The success of these elaborate productions motivated New York's then newly burgeoning theater culture to stage not one, but two *Dream* productions in February 1854. These over-the-top versions used machinery to manipulate the props and actors through phases of the moon, an opening sun, an elevator that lifted Puck up on a mushroom out of the cellarage through a trap door, and a moving and elevated platform that carried Oberon and Titania into the sunrise.

In 1900, Herbert Beerbohm Tree (1853–1917) used live animals on stage, creating scenery that was not always under the control of the director or the actors. Towards the end of the nineteenth century, the innovative director William Poel (1852–1934) tried to bring something of the Elizabethan stage back to Shakespeare's plays, and by the early twentieth century, Harley Granville Barker (1877–1946), acknowledging Poel's influence, created a *Dream* at the Savoy Theater in 1912–14 that eliminated most of the Romantic and Victorian innovations, restoring the text and eliminating the elaborate scenery as well as cutting Mendelssohn's music in favor of English folk tunes. By the early twentieth century, the presentation of Shakespeare's plays began to focus on the drama instead of the "show." We owe Madame Vestris for her understanding of the possibilities of the text and for experimenting with new setting possibilities, William Poel for daring to reject nineteenth century theatrical conventions in his quest to reclaim Shakespeare's stage, and Granville Barker for resurrecting that most vital aspect of performing Shakespeare: a reliance on language rather than opulent scenery and music to convey the dream and emphasize the centrality of the human imagination in Shakespeare.

THE TWENTIETH CENTURY AND MODERN INTERPRETATION

World War I, World War II, and the destruction of old Europe and European traditions had its inevitable effect on theater culture. The ravages of two wars and the threat of nuclear annihilation left playwrights (and other creative artists) wondering what was happening to human culture, the environment, and mythological and religious belief systems. Long-established traditions, conventions, and values were called into question. Shakespeare's plays were reinterpreted in light of the effects of modern nihilism, pessimism, and doubt. Technology was changing the world faster then artists could adapt and it took some time before all of these elements began to be integrated into new interpretations of plays, including *A Midsummer Night's Dream.* Art eventually emerged as a haven for aesthetics and a way to transcend the horrors and uncertainties of a mechanized society. Between World War I and World War II, productions of *The Dream* fluctuated between the nineteenth century tradition of dancing fairies and nearly vaudevillian Mechanicals and Mendelssohn, and simpler, more "Elizabethan" interpretations. After that, however, the changing world and the uncertainty of the political and economic situations would alter presentations in ways that most nineteenth century directors could not have imagined.

Max Reinhardt's Dream

In 1935, just as Nazi Germany was making itself felt on the political horizon, the Austrian director Max Reinhardt (1873–1943) would bring *A Midsummer Night's Dream* to that iconic venue of the twentieth century, the cinema. Reinhardt began his career on the stage but it was behind the scenes where he built his reputation, becoming known as a prolific and innovative director. He saw the theater as a place where the cultural community could experience "richness and abundance" and was determined to bring exactly that to his audiences. He cast his plays with experienced, well-known actors and used a combination of romanticism and modernism in all of his stagings. His forest, central to all of his productions of *The Dream,* came from Germanic folklore and from the Black Forest of the Brothers Grimm. Reinhardt's forest operated as an entity around, in, and through which Shakespeare's play moved. He relied heavily on Mendelssohn's score whether he was working with a stage production or his film.

In 1934, Reinhardt was invited to stage *A Midsummer Night's Dream* at three venues, including the Hollywood Bowl. Because of the success of his lavish productions, Jack Warner offered him a contract to bring the play to film. Reinhardt, assisted by William Dieterle, made the first full-length film adaptation of Shakespeare's *Dream.* The film (143 minutes) stands as a testament to Reinhardt's vision, replete with a strong Hollywood cast including Mickey Rooney (Puck), James Cagney (Bottom), Olivia DeHavilland (Hermia), Joe E. Brown (Thisbe), Victor Jory (Oberon), Mendelssohn's music, and revolutionary cinematic techniques. The film is shot in black-and-white, but instead of detracting from the color of the play as one might expect, it adds an interesting

The performance of *Pyramus and Thisbe*, from Reinhardt's film
Courtesy: Douglas Lanier

contrast that emphasizes the silver-black and moonlit forest and the garishly bright and gaudy court. Oberon's twinkling black cloak seems as endless as the boundaries of space and Bronislava Nijinska's ballet is a delicate reminder of the fragility of beauty in a world grown threatening. While the film received some critical praise, it was neither popular with filmgoers nor profitable at the box office. Since the movie cost over $1.5 million to film (double the expected budget), Reinhardt was not offered further movie contracts.

The Forward Momentum of Peter Hall and the Royal Shakespeare Company

The immutability of the text transcended the chaos of a changing world and it remained an integral part of the cultural-artistic experience—until Hall and Brook. On stage, *The Dream* continued to challenge directors to make it relevant to the new world that emerged after World War II. George Devine (1910–1965), who founded the English Stage Company in London's Royal Court Theater in 1956, staged a colorful science fiction version of *A Midsummer Night's Dream* at Stratford in 1954. Perhaps in reaction to Devine,

Peter Hall (1930–), who founded the Royal Shakespeare Company (RSC) in Stratford in 1960, staged *The Dream* with his new company in 1961. Hall's production reclaimed Shakespeare's forest/court setting but, influenced by the work of the famed Polish theater critic and theoretician Jan Kott (1914–2001), Hall challenged the audience to participate in a new vision of Shakespeare. Hall, a contemporary of Peter Brook, was also influenced by Bertolt Brecht's (1898–1956) belief in the ability of the audience to interpret drama through the actions of the actors. A-Effect (or "alienation effect") intended to focus the audience's attention on the individual characters rather then the overall story. Hall moved away from the centrality of the text and looked for a deeper meaning—a meaning more relevant than simply the words could convey. In his stage production of *The Dream,* Hall combined Elizabethan conventions and illusion, or abstract dream elements, to create the feeling that the fairy world existed alongside of and just beneath the consciousness of the Court. Hall eliminated the use of a complete ass's head for Bottom in favor of a simple set of ears growing from his head and a pair of hooves on his hands. Judi Dench played Titania in a costume consisting only of green paint and leaves, and the entire staging carried a distinctively modernist stamp—in spite of the English Tudor garden setting. This production formed the basis for Hall's 1969 film adaptation, purposely filmed on dreary, rainy days. The characters play their roles in a foggy, wet world, emphasizing the vagaries of the forest and the confusion and foolishness of their lives. The fairies and attendants always have an unkempt, dirty look about them, as if nature challenges them as much as it challenges the humans. For the film, Hall made the surprising choice to transform Bottom with a complete ass's head instead of leaving his face openly human. Still, everything about Hall's film stands in opposition to adaptations like Reinhardt's. Hall's innovations, especially the deeply psychological interpretation where uncontrolled sexuality and irrationality vie for supremacy over conventional and rational behavior, redefined Shakespeare. He seems to ask, what is illusion and what is the nature of reality?

Peter Brook's Dream

Peter Brook (1925–), like his contemporary, Peter Hall, was also influenced by Kott. With a strong conviction that the authority of art lies in the power of the audience's imagination, Brook staged *A Midsummer Night's Dream* for the RSC in Stratford in 1970. It is generally recognized to be the definitive production of the twentieth century. Inspired by the modernist minimalist movements in art and literature, he did away with the forest and the court, using only a white box with invisible "tiring house" doors, ladders, and a catwalk from which musicians and fairies could interact with the action below. Brook compared this stage set to a circus. Just as a Shakespearean audience would have been familiar with the fairies in the forest and would have looked upon them as purveyors of magic and tricks, an audience in the cultural milieu of the twentieth century would recognize such an environment in the circus. Brook's set seems to have been the modern equivalent of Puck's woods. Brook made other daring choices in his production: Bottom and Titania come together in open sexuality—there are no vague allusions or suggestions. He doubled the roles of Theseus and Oberon, Hippolyta and Titania, and Philostrate and Puck, casting single actors in these dual roles, cementing the links between the fairy world and the world of the court. Such casting choices are now common. "Brook's *Dream,*" as it is called, has exerted a powerful influence on subsequent productions of the play. (For more on this *Dream,* see Peter Holland's essay "As Performed" in this book.)

The Mechanicals rehearsing in the forest, from Peter Brook's 1970 *Dream*
Royal Shakespeare Library

We owe Max Reinhardt for providing a *Dream* that gives us a glimpse of what nineteenth century romantic productions looked like as well as a glimpse into the direction art would have to take to adjust to film and the post-war world. We owe Peter Hall for founding the RSC and for staging a production that would move Shakespeare and *The Dream* into the latter part of the twentieth century. And we owe Peter Brook for bringing Shakespeare's vision, so alive in the drama of *The Dream*, to a world where visions and dreams are far too often disregarded or remain unrealized.

THE ARTISTIC AND COMMERCIAL FUTURE OF THE *Dream* ON STAGE AND FILM

Just as *A Midsummer Night's Dream* is one of the most frequently staged of Shakespeare's plays, so it is one of the plays most frequently adapted to film. In fact, *The Dream* can be considered one of the most filmable of Shakespeare's plays, since it offers opportunities for filmic and theatric moments as well as realism. The camera can act as an eye, focusing in on those things the director deems most valuable. Fairies can fly, appear and disappear, and change their outward appearance entirely. These qualities seem to have been recognized early on by those artists captivated by the possibilities inherent in the new medium of film. The first live-action film, an eight-minute adaptation of Puck and several fairies cavorting in New York's Central Park, was released in 1908. In 1925, Hans Neumann produced a fifty-minute film of *The Dream,* but it was censored for nudity and sexuality.

After Max Reinhardt's 1935 film, *A Midsummer Night's Dream* was not filmed again until Peter Hall's 1968 cinematic version of his RSC production. Perhaps the failure of Reinhardt's film at the box office dissuaded other filmmakers from attempting to produce it. Adrian Noble directed the *The Dream* in 1996 with the RSC and Guild Films. Noble experimented with and emphasized the ability of the actors to communicate the reality of illusion to the audience—just as Puck asks us to do in Shakespeare's epilogue. Unlike Brook's dark interpretation, Noble sees the play—and interprets the play—through the eyes of a child. One of his central images is the use of parasols, umbrellas, and Quince's bumbershoot. The value of Noble's production is that, while using Brook's example of trusting the imagination, it simultaneously delivers a message that film interpretations of stage action can translate to film without losing that which makes them imaginative.

The most recent film adaptation of *A Midsummer Night's Dream* (with the exception of Christine Edzard's 2001 *The Children's Midsummer Night's Dream*, cast entirely with children and directed towards them) is Michael Hoffman's 1999 Fox Searchlight star-studded production with Kevin Kline as Bottom, Michelle Pfeiffer as Titania, Rupert Everett as Oberon, Calista Flockhart as Helena, and Stanley Tucci as Puck. This production, quite removed from Brook, uses an Italian landscape, and, overlaid with the music of Mendelssohn, Verdi, and Rossini, attempts to reinforce the audience's belief in the magic of love and the power of imagination.

The Future of Dream

Brook created an exciting awareness of the possibilities inherent in the imagination, and his production dares other directors to stage Shakespeare's plays in innovative ways. Neo-romanticism will still exist and Mendelssohn will continue to play as fairies dance, but after Hall and Brook, new possibilities are available to directors who want to experiment with a play that asks us to think about illusion, the nature of theater, and the willingness of the audience to join in the dance wholeheartedly.

The *Dream* that Shakespeare had in his own time is as pertinent to the twenty-first century stage as it was to a sixteenth century audience. The fact that Peter Hall and Peter Brook chose this play as a medium through which they were able to demonstrate their radical new theatrical techniques stands as a testament to its power and durability. As theater continues to adapt to a changing world brought about by political, cultural, and linguistic boundary shifts, and as different kinds of stages arise from yet unimaginable technologies, *A Midsummer Night's Dream* will play a major role in the way we reinterpret Shakespeare. Perhaps of all of his plays, *Dream* can perhaps best realize the essence of what makes theater, and the capabilities inherent in the human imagination.

As Performed

By The Royal Shakespeare Company at
Stratford-upon-Avon in 1970

Peter Holland

"Once in a while," writes Clive Barnes, the leading New York theater critic, "once in a very rare while, a theatrical production arrives that is going to be talked about as long as there is a theater, a production, which, for good or ill, is going to exert a major influence on the contemporary stage…If Peter Brook had done nothing else but this *Dream,* he would have deserved a place in theater history."

I, for one, have not stopped talking about Brook's *A Midsummer Night's Dream* since, and I remember vividly the experience of seeing the production in the autumn of 1970, now thirty-five years ago, recalling not only the details of the performance but above all the emotions it fired in me. Driving a hundred miles to Stratford-upon-Avon to see a matinee, I was running late, couldn't find a parking spot and left the car where I was sure it would be ticketed. Settling into my seat three minutes before curtain-up I could not imagine why I had wanted to see this most childish of Shakespeare's plays. I came out three hours later dancing, filled with more joy than any other theater performance has given me, before or since. Whatever else Brook had achieved in the past, he seemed at that moment to have reinvented the play, the possibilities of performing Shakespeare, and the forms of Western theater. There are choices I now might disagree with, but the scale of the achievement is plain. *A Midsummer Night's Dream* could not belong to the world of gossamer and tutus, the Victorian sensibility and a narrow conception of theater ever again. Classical theater—and Shakespeare in particular—would never be the same.

If some of the methods now seem part of theater's vocabulary, they were startling then. Where Shakespeare productions had tended, to a greater or lesser extent, towards a kind of representational world, a set that pointed towards a fictive location for the action, costume designs that hinted at or defined a historical moment, and techniques that belonged unequivocally to the conventions of classical theater, Brook replaced them or, better, conjoined them with ideas drawn from radically different traditions. John Kane, who played Puck, was, to say the least, surprised when Sally Jacobs, the production's designer, showed him her sketch of his costume,

> …a drawing of a curly-headed character wearing a one-piece-baggy-panted-luminous-yellow-jumpsuit and a moonlight-blue skullcap. I found it impossible to relate the picture I held in my hand to any conception I may have had of the part of "Puck" up to that time. Peter [Brook] explained.
>
> Recently both he and Sally had witnessed a Chinese circus in Paris and had been struck by the different between our performers and theirs. When the occidental acrobat performs, his costume emphasizes his physique…Peter's Chinese acrobats hid the shape of their bodies with long flowing silk robes and performed their tricks with delicacy and speed, so that it seemed the most natural thing in the world for them to spin plates, or walk on stilts.

With that experience in mind and with the intention of importing this style to the play's fairy world, Brook and Jacobs rethought the whole way in which the wood and the fairies' actions could be presented. No longer a matter of representation, instead objects became symbolic of the concepts to which they alluded. What does a magic flower look like? It can be a plant representing whatever botanical specimen a director believes to be the true form of "love-in-idleness" (2.1.168) but that never seems especially magical. Bringing the flower to Oberon (Alan Howard), Kane's Puck entered (2.1.246), high above the stage, swinging on a trapeze; his response to "Hast thou the flower there?" was to reach into his pocket and take out a silver plate, spin it on the end of a clear, plastic rod and tip it to Oberon who took it, still spinning, on a similar rod, all accompanied by the eerie sound of a finger running round the rim of a wineglass. As Peter Thomson, reviewing the production in *Shakespeare Survey,* puts it, "the plate does not *become* the flower. Instead, the act of passing it becomes the *magic* of the flower."

Puck (John Kane, on stilts) chases Lysander (Christopher Gable, left) and Demetrius (Ben Kingsley)
around the forest
Royal Shakespeare Company

In such a world, there could be no leafy trees; instead the fairies—here adult actors, three men and one woman, often malevolent spirits and known to the company as the Audio-Visuals since they made strange sounds and moved objects around—dropped great coils of wire, like giant Slinkies, enmeshing Hermia when she woke from her dream in these mobile but resisting cages. Here Titania's bower became a gigantic red ostrich feather suspended over the stage. Here the sounds of the forest were bangs and crashes, rasps and rattles, and, above all, the strange whoosh of Free-kas, plastic tubes that the fairies whirled to produce pitched but undefined and certainly unearthly noises. It was no surprise that these fairies sang Titania to sleep by sitting cross-legged on trapezes singing a distinctly Indian chant, like spirits from a world much visited by 60s hippies. As well as magic, these fairies became comic helpers: when Bottom calls for a calendar to "find out moonshine" (3.1.39), a fairy threw one down to him; when Bottom is still asleep, alone on stage, at the end of the forest scenes (4.1), a fairy arm appeared from the side of the stage holding out an alarm clock ringing his wake-up call.

The fairies and a slumbering Titania (Sara Kestelman) in her bower
Royal Shakespeare Company

The stage space itself had no hint of palace or forest in its set design. The action took place on, above, and around a giant white box, as if the characters were trapped in a squash court, its unyielding harshness setting off the bright colors of the costumes and making the long night in the wood, in this greatest of all comedies of the night, something we imagined rather than something we saw conjured up by the effects of stage lighting. Twelve feet above the stage floor, on the top of the three sides of the box, ran a platform where actors not in a scene stood and watched, laughed and made noises, at times participating in the action but always, like us, observing it, sharing the spectacle of performance. There was no question: the onstage watchers were actors as well as characters, admirers of their colleagues' circus skills, their lyric verse-speaking, or their exuberance.

If little of this seemed to have links to the ways *A Midsummer Night's Dream* had usually been played for the previous century or so, the production was perfectly capable of conjuring up the play's performance history. In Brook's theater, love was not a platonic emotion divorced from the sharpness of sexual desire. Titania's love for the transformed Bottom was unquestionably the desire for sex with him and, though she spoke the line "Tie up my lover's tongue, bring him silently" (3.1.171), the moment was anything but silent. Instead, Bottom, braying like an ass, hoisted on a fairy's shoulder with the fairy's arm raised as an erect donkey phallus between his legs, left the stage triumphantly, with the watchers throwing dozens of paper-plates and streamers, Oberon swinging from side to side on a trapeze, equally triumphant in his revenge on his erring Queen, and, at massive volume, the sound of Mendelssohn's "Wedding March," originally written as part of his incidental music to the play, blaring in ironic solemnity on this impossible and lust-filled "marriage." No longer the sound for the Athenian triple-wedding, the march now celebrated the complex meanings of this act of love.

The fairies (Ralph Cotterill and John York) carry Bottom (David Waller) to Titania (Sara Kestelman) Royal Shakespeare Company

There had been radical departures from tradition in earlier productions of *A Midsummer Night's Dream:* Harley Granville Barker in 1914 had his fairies wear gold-leaf makeup, making them gilded exotics; George Devine in 1954 turned the fairy world into an assemblage of strange beasts and birds, threatening and disturbing. But Brook's project was to find the play's heart, its thematic unity, not by finding the right analog external to the theater but instead by celebrating theater itself. The answers lay within the space of the rehearsal room, not by the imposition of an external concept. In the white box, with these colorful abstract costumes, to the strange palette of music and sounds created by Richard Peaslee, the production could be an apparently limitless investigation, a free examination of what might be found in the play. In *The Shifting Point*, Brook writes that "at the center of the *Dream,* constantly repeated, we find the word 'love,'" but at the center of the production lay the collaborative manifestation of imagination that is theater. If *A Midsummer Night's Dream* had seemed to be the Shakespeare play best for children, the meaning of that now lay not in a cute exposition of an adult's view of fairies but instead through the reinvestment of the play with the qualities of the child's imagination, sometimes happy, often troubled, always ranging unexpectedly across the playfulness of all play and plays.

It was not exactly the most probable route for Brook. Born in 1925, Peter Brook was directing in Stratford-upon-Avon very soon after graduating from Oxford, helming *Love's Labour's Lost* (1946) and *Romeo and Juliet* (1947). As he approached the production of *A Midsummer Night's Dream,* he had just finished editing his film of *King Lear,* a bleak vision powerfully defined by Beckett and Brecht and strongly influenced (as his stage production of the play for the Royal Shakespeare Company in 1962 had been) by the work of the Polish Shakespeare critic Jan Kott. His stage version of Peter Weiss's *Marat/Sade* (RSC, 1964, filmed 1966) and the devised anti-Vietnam show *US* (RSC, 1966, filmed 1967) were both terrifying political visions, and neither show suggested that a Brook production of *A Midsummer Night's Dream* would contain any joy or lightness. What it did show, though, was that Brook's search for the possibilities of theater was going ever deeper. With his version of Seneca's *Oedipus* for the National Theatre in London (1968) and the experiments with *The Tempest* (The Roundhouse, 1968), more a series of exercises than a production of the play, Brook had started to engage other forms of performance far from classical theater.

It is one of the central paradoxes of Brook's version of *A Midsummer Night's Dream* that this, the most beautifully spoken production of the play I have ever heard, was accomplished without the director giving the actors any textual notes at all. The rehearsal room was a space to develop physical skills (stilt-walking, juggling), not to work on the actors' voices. The rhythm of the lyric verse was found through the actors' bodies, the musical score, and the interaction of characters, not through close attention to the iambic pentameter and the extraordinary range of other meters Shakespeare uses in the play.

What emerged from this play-space was the utter seriousness of the business of making theater. Indeed, the accounts of the rehearsal process (especially in David Selbourne's day-by-day diary of the weeks of work, *The Making of "A Midsummer Night's Dream"*) are often descriptions of actors in despair. Brook's outbursts of anger at their failure to find new modes of performance drove the actors further and further into a space of insecurity.

If the preparation was for some traumatic and others revelatory, it transferred something of both outcomes into the play's most complete investigation of the making of theater, the workers' performance of *Pyramus and Thisbe*. Where productions have usually treated this as the opportunity for endless gags, unlimited mockery, and a contempt shared between the onstage and theater spectators, Brook showed utter respect for their endeavors. Still funny, they could be moving as well. Lysander's comment on the death of

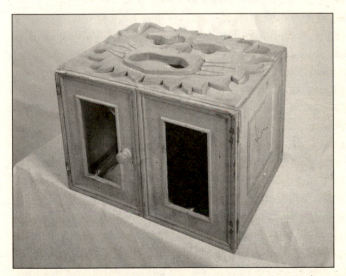

The Lion's Head as designed by Sally Jacobs and worn by Snug the Joiner (Barry Stanton)
Royal Shakespeare Company

Pyramus, "Less than an ace, man, for he is dead. He is nothing" (5.1.289), dropped into a silence born not of mockery but of desolation at the confrontation with mortality. Perhaps nothing typified this serious comedy more than the lion's mask, a wooden cabinet that Snug had made as a skilled carpenter (he is a "joiner" after all), with its front suggesting a lion's face but with two neat doors that he could open to show his own face within in order to reassure the "ladies" who might otherwise "quake and tremble here" (5.1.209-211). His pride and skill in his trade glowed over any inadequacies he might display as actor.

In effect, Brook shared Theseus's understanding of the workers' play, that there is no fundamental separation between their amateur efforts and the performance of consummate professionals: "The best in this kind are but shadows; and the worst are no worse, if imagination amend them" (5.1.203-204). All are engaged in the same ambition, to find in theater a means of communication of ideas and emotions, thoughts and possibilities beyond the quotidian. If the workers have "never labored in their minds till now" (5.1.73), their aim is the same as the performers in Brook's production and the latter are just as likely to fail to communicate their art.

One of the most imitated of Brook's devices has been the doubling of Titania and Hippolyta, Oberon and Theseus, and Puck and Philostrate. On the one hand, the doubling suggests a thematic meaning, that the experiences of the night in the wood are a kind of dream-projection; the tension caused by the prenuptial anxiety of the rulers is lessened in this alternate world of the forest. But, on the other hand, the doubling in Brook's version is less a meaning-laden statement and more a spectacle enjoyable for its theatrical virtuosity. Confronted with the rapid change from fairy world to human world at 4.1.97 where Fairy King and Queen exit and Athenian Duke and future Duchess enter immediately, Brook's solution was, as throughout the production, to make the mechanics of the transformation, the reality of performance, completely visible. The two actors walked upstage in one role, then turned and walked downstage in the other, donning cloaks to define the difference. The doubling is not a problem for theater: if we accept Alan Howard and Sarah Kestelman as one pair we can equally accept them as the other a moment later. As Jay Halio comments in Manchester University Press's 1995 offering *A Midsummer Night's Dream*, "What had once been regarded as a difficult if not impossible doubling now looks, thanks to imaginative and simple staging, perfectly natural." It is the collocation of "imaginative and simple" that defines Brook's method, turning what seems intellectually problematic into the easily acceptable theatrical solution by rethinking theater to its essence.

Shakespeare's play ends with Puck's request for applause: "Give us your hands, if we be friends" (Epilogue, line 15). Brook's actors, having played out the last sequence of the play in a downbeat way, did not ask us to clap but instead to reach out our hands and grasp theirs as they left the stage and moved among us (and John Kane could be heard up in the circle calling "Author, author!" when I saw it). For the one and only time in my playgoing, I did reach out my hands, not threatened by the breaking of the barriers between actors and audience but instead thrilled to be able to join with them physically, as we had all joined together throughout the performance. As Brook wrote in *The Empty Space*, "there is only a practical difference between actor and audience, not a fundamental one."

After *A Midsummer Night's Dream*, Brook left England, spending two years taking productions across Africa before establishing his Centre for International Theatre Research in Paris soon after. He has kept returning to Shakespeare, with productions of *Timon of Athens, The Tempest*, and *Hamlet,* for example, all brilliant, revisionary and thrilling, though his only subsequent production for the Royal Shakespeare Company was *Antony and Cleopatra* in 1978. If I always regret that only tiny fragments of his *Dream* were filmed, it also seems only right that this most theatrical of productions was never transferred to another medium. Instead, the still photos recall this energetic production, memories preserve traces of its sound, and the production goes on being talked about.

"That You Have but Slumbered Here"

A Midsummer Night's Dream IN POPULAR CULTURE

Douglas Lanier

Though *A Midsummer Night's Dream* has become one of Shakespeare's most beloved comedies, it was not always so. Throughout the later seventeenth century and much of the eighteenth, *Midsummer* was widely regarded as minor Shakespeare, and it was rarely staged by the legitimate theaters of the day. When diarist Samuel Pepys saw the play soon after the reopening of the theaters in 1662, he dubbed it "the most insipid ridiculous play that ever I saw in my life," a judgment apparently shared by many others. (Pepys goes on to add that "I saw, I confess, some good dancing and some handsome women, which was all my pleasure," pointing toward the atmosphere of sensuality with which the play was later identified.)

DROLLS AND MUSIC

Until the nineteenth century, *A Midsummer Night's Dream* appeared before audiences primarily in two forms. One is the "droll," a short play long on farce, slapstick, and punning that would be performed at fair booths, taverns, and the like. *The Merry Conceits of Bottom the Weaver,* first published in 1646, splices together passages from Shakespeare's play involving Bottom into the theatrical equivalent of his greatest hits. The eighteenth century also saw a vogue for operatic adaptations of *A Midsummer Night's Dream,* a trend begun by Henry Purcell with his opera *The Fairy Queen* (1692) and followed by several others in the next one hundred years. Some adaptors even used the Mechanicals' play as a platform for parodying Italian opera, an approach revived in the twentieth century by Benjamin Britten in his opera *A Midsummer Night's Dream* (1960). As Gary Jay Williams observes in his fine overview of the play's stage history, *Midsummer*'s mythological, earthy, erotic, and fanciful elements were ill-suited to the dominant rationalism and neoclassical tastes of the eighteenth century, and so music served as an appropriate vehicle for its mix of fantasy and foolery. The impulse to adapt *A Midsummer Night's Dream* to musical form remains strong, though none has been successful with the general public. At the height of popularity of swing, *Swingin' the Dream* (1939), an ambitious jazz adaptation, appeared briefly on Broadway. The roster of luminaries involved in the production is breathtaking: to name a few, Benny Goodman played in the band, Agnes DeMille directed the choreography, "Moms" Mabley and Butterfly McQueen sang, and Louis Armstrong played Puck. Later musical theater versions— *Babes in the Wood* (1964), *The Dream on Royal Street* (1981), *Midsummer Nights* (1989), *Another Midsummer Night* (1995), *Dream Nights* (1997), *A Midsummer Night's Dream: The Rock Musical* (1999), and *The Dreaming* (2003)—have, despite their adaptational ingenuity, similarly failed to find a wide audience.

Despite the lack of success of musical adaptations of the play, music has made a lasting contribution to its adaptational history. Felix Mendelssohn's incidental music for *A Midsummer Night's Dream,* written in 1843 for a Prussian production of the play, was immediately popular and has remained indelibly linked to the play ever since. It has been especially associated with dance versions of the play, having been used as the score for the dance sequences in Max Reinhardt and William Dieterle's 1935 film adaptation and as the score for George Balanchine's 1962 and Frederick Ashton's 1964 ballet versions of the play. Two pieces by noted pop composers, *Il Sogno* (2004), a orchestral score for a ballet by Elvis Costello, and *A Midsummer Night's Dream* (2003), an orchestral suite by ex Genesis guitarist Steve Hackett, follow in a similar vein. Though relatively few may recognize its Shakespearean associations, Mendelssohn's "Wedding March," a tune written to announce the triple marriage of the Athenians, has become a standard musical accompaniment for bridal couples as they walk to take their vows.

MUSIC INSPIRED BY *A Midsummer Night's Dream*

Mendelssohn's *A Midsummer Night's Dream* (1843)	incidental music written for a Prussian production
Mendelssohn's *A Wedding March* (1843)	tune written to announce the triple marriage of the Athenians
Elvis Costello's *Il Sogno* (2004)	orchestral score for ballet
Steve Hackett's *A Midsummer Night's Dream* (2003)	orchestral suite

FOLKLORE, FERTILITY, AND FANCIES

The play's popular fortunes changed dramatically with the emergence of the Romantic movement in the early nineteenth century. For several reasons the Romantics found *Midsummer* more amenable to their philosophies and artistic taste. The folk origins of the Mechanicals and fairies accorded with the Romantic interest in the traditional culture of the rural British commons. The play's focus on Nature's beauty and fertility, especially in evidence in its lush descriptive passages, found a receptive audience among the Romantics, who often made the natural world the subject of their art. And Shakespeare's strong emphasis on the power of the imagination, famously summarized in Theseus's speech on "lovers, madmen and poets" in 5.1, resonated with the Romantics' praise of "fancy," those imaginative, non-rational states of mind such as dream, intoxication, and reverie so integral to Romantic conceptions of artistic creation and genius. The works of two visual artists of the age, William Blake and Henry Fuseli, epitomize this shift in perception of the play. William Blake's two illustrations of the play (both dating from the 1780s) feature Titania and Oberon, in one as charming figures nestled in a lily, in the other as a loving couple presiding over a dance of the fairies. In the last decade of the eighteenth century, Fuseli painted several striking images of Bottom, Titania, and Titania's fairy

Bottom, surrounded by Titania and the fairies, by Henry Fuseli
Mary Evans Picture Library

attendants. In them he pictures Bottom as a musclebound, ass-headed mon-
strosity in a stolid pose, Titania as an ethereal young beauty gracefully
orchestrating a teeming swirl of fairies, animals, and vegetation. Fuseli's
images illustrate the triumph of the dreamlike imagination over brutish
rationality, natural fertility over mechanical modernity, sensuality and love
over workaday mundane life. Fuseli's are among the most compelling and
influential illustrations of *A Midsummer Night's Dream* ever produced.

A Focus on Fairies

These artists' focus on supernatural creatures presages the preoccupations of adaptors who followed them. Of the three groups of characters featured in *A Midsummer Night's Dream*—the Athenians, the Mechanicals, and the fairies—it is the fairies who have most fired the post-Romantic imagination and inspired popular adaptations well into the twentieth century. *A Midsummer Night's Dream* is closely associated with the Victorian fascination with fairy lore, a fascination which extended not only to fairy painting (the painters Sir Joseph Noel Paton and Richard Dadd often returned to *Midsummer* for inspiration) but also to book illustration, music, household kitsch, and lavish nineteenth century stagings of the play. Whereas for Shakespeare's first audiences the Titania, Oberon, and Bottom plotline might have played as a send-up of the cult of Elizabeth I, the Virgin Queen, and the institution of royal favorite, for latter-day audiences Shakespeare's fairies became largely apolitical figures, associated primarily with natural fertility, sensuality, magic, and an innocence unsullied by civilization.

Puck, the changeling, and Titania from an engraving by Edward Scriven, circa 1815
Mary Evans Picture Library

Fairies and Sentimentalism

After the Victorian age depictions of fairies generally took one of two directions in popular culture, both of which influenced pop appropriations of *Midsummer.* One is sentimentalization. In many depictions fairies became childlike magical creatures, in effect secularized cherubs, often depicted in an idealized Nature heavy on whimsy and charm.

Reinhardt and Dieterle's 1935 film partakes of this tradition, using Victorian fairy painting as one of its central points of reference. One measure of this approach's influence may be found in the depiction of Titania and Bottom's relationship, which has increasingly come to be regarded as the play's centerpiece. Instead of presenting this relationship as threatening or comical, many adaptations portray it as deeply (but innocently) romantic or vaguely maternal. The cover of the *Classics Illustrated* comic adaptation (#87), produced in 1951, offers a good example. In a moonlit forest, a somewhat mature Titania, dressed in a fetching, quasi-classical robe, places a wreath on Bottom's head as he clasps his hands in infantile delight; as she does so, childlike fairies emerge from the thick woodland greenery. Below, we see an Athenian asleep in the grass, the scalloped edges of the image suggesting that the image of Titania and Bottom is his dream, even though his clothing clearly indicates that he is not Bottom. Shakespeare's pointed satire of a romance between an ass and a queen has been replaced with a sentimental treatment of their love, a trend also at work in popular citations of Titania and Bottom's dialogue. A 2005 commercial for Levi's jeans features a young man in modern dress walking the mean streets of Los Angeles at night as he recites Bottom's speech about not showing his fear (3.1), all without any indication of the ironic tone of Shakespeare's original. At ad's end, a fetching young woman comments, with admiration, on his jeans: "Mine eye is enthralled to thy shape."

Adaptations for and about Children

Closely akin to the Victorian sentimentalizing of fairies is their depiction as infantile creatures, a portrayal which strongly influenced pop culture and through it *A Midsummer Night's Dream.* This trend helps explains why the play has become so closely associated with children and children's literature. Tellingly, *A Midsummer Night's Dream* is the Shakespeare play most often adapted to children's book form. Film adaptations have embraced that association in different ways. Max Reinhardt and William Dieterle's 1935 film casts a young Mickey Rooney as an impish, childlike Puck with an unforgettable manic laugh, and also portrays Titania and Oberon as Puck's surrogate parents; Adrian Noble's 1996 adaptation reimagines the play as a child's Freudian dream about his parents and builds in allusions to such children's classics as *The Wizard of Oz* and *Alice in Wonderland;* and Christine Edzard's 2001 film features an all-children cast in a lavish production which pays homage to Victorian staging and fairy lore. Perhaps the film that best exemplifies this adaptational strain is Jirí Trnka's *A Midsummer Night's Dream* (1959), an extraordinary but now largely forgotten film by the noted Czech animator. Trnka tells Shakespeare's tale with charming puppets and virtuoso stop-action animation, emphasizing the childlike innocence of Shakespeare's characters as well as the technological "magic" of Trnka's medium. The recent Spanish animated adaptation *Midsummer Dream* (2005, directed by Ángel de la Cruz and Manolo Gómez) follows somewhat less successfully in Trnka's footsteps.

The "cast" of Trnka's 1959 production
Courtesy: Douglas Lanier

Fairies and Sensuality

It is rather ironic that *A Midsummer Night's Dream* is widely regarded as a work for children, for the other strand of the modern portrayal of fairies emphasizes their sexual appeal, in essence bringing to the surface qualities implicit in Victorian fairy lore. Accordingly, Shakespeare's play has also become associated in the popular imagination with erotic abandon, an understandable association given that myriad romantic couplings and uncouplings happen in the fairy wood in the course of a single evening. It is not accidental that *A Midsummer Night's Dream* is the Shakespearean play most frequently alluded to in pornographic film titles, for the reference seems to promise an erotic idyll and considerable sexual variety. This association also clarifies why an annual party given at the Playboy Mansion in Los Angeles would be labeled "A Midsummer Night's Dream." Fairy sensuality dominates, for example, Michael Hoffman's portrayal of the fairies in his 1999 film adaptation. In stark contrast to the buttoned-up and corseted Athenians who wander into the wood, Titania's attendants bathe in the nude, lounge in diaphanous garments, and enjoy culinary delicacies. By visually alluding to Pre-Raphaelite paintings with his sexy fairy sequences, Hoffman pays homage to the link between Victorian iconographic traditions and the sensuality of *A Midsummer Night's Dream*.

EROTICISM AND MODERN ROMANTIC COMEDY

The association between *Midsummer* and eroticism also lies behind its occasional use as a point of reference in modern romantic comedy. Ingmar Bergman's film *Smiles of a Summer Night* (1955) adopts a number of motifs from Shakespeare's play—a pastoral setting, mismatched couples, a magic potion, the removal of romantic illusion—to underline the timelessness of his theme of male erotic misperception. Woody Allen's *A Midsummer Night's Sex Comedy* (1982) recasts Bergman's film so that its debts to *A Midsummer Night's Dream* are much clearer. In addition to the Shakespearean motifs Bergman adapts, Allen opens with a lecture on rationalism from Leopold, the story's patriarch, that obliquely alludes to Theseus's "lovers, madmen and poets" speech, and Leopold later offers a toast that directly cites Titania's description of the fairy royals' quarrel from 2.1. As if to drive home the association, the film liberally quotes from Mendelssohn's score. More recently, *A Midsummer Night's Dream* has been used in a similar fashion in youth culture adaptations. *A Midsummer Night's Rave* (2001, directed by Gil Cates) transposes the play's action to a drug- and flirt-filled rave party, though it significantly replots Shakespeare's narrative to accommodate a homosexual relationship and to allow one liberated woman, Elena, to reject her callow lover. Nostalgia for casual drugs and free sexuality (as well as the "magic" of the 70s glam lifestyle) suffuses the off-Broadway stage extravaganza *The Donkey Show* (1999, written by Ralph Weiner), which sets a dialogueless adaptation of Shakespeare's play in the heyday of disco and reconceives the fairies as extravagantly-dressed club regulars. *Get Over It* (2001, directed by Tommy O'Haver), a more conventional teen comedy in the style of *10 Things I Hate About You* or *Never Been Kissed,* uses a musical production of *A Midsummer Night's Dream* as the armature for the tale of a teen boy, Berke, recovering from a painful breakup. Berke's recurrent fantasy sequences in the film are set in a golden-lit Athenian wood in which he, like Lysander, vies with his rival, Striker, for the affections of Allison, his former girlfriend. Interestingly, in the end Berke simply rewrites Shakespeare's plot so that he ends up with Kelly, his costar. Actors' romances paralleling those of their characters are a well-worn motif in Shakespearean adaptations. In this vein, Marilyn Singer's *The Course of True Love Never Did Run Smooth* (1983), a young adult novel in which offstage romance becomes intertwined with onstage performances, anticipates *Get Over It* by nearly twenty years. "Midsummer Night's Dream" (1994), the second episode of the Japanese anime series *Oh, My Goddess!,* offers yet another variation on this theme. In the series, Keichi, a shy university student, is involved in an everunconsummated relationship with the goddess Belldandy, a situation which bears some resemblance to that of Bottom and Titania. In this particular episode, Belldandy's evil sister Urd uses a love potion to encourage a sexual spark between the two.

Movies Inspired By *A Midsummer Night's Dream*

Ingmar Bergman's *Smiles of a Summer Night* (1955)	adopts motifs from the play including: pastoral setting, mismatched couples, a magic potion, removal of romantic illusion
Woody Allen's *A Midsummer Night's Sex Comedy* (1982)	uses Bergman motifs as well as allusions to speeches from the play and quotes Mendelssohn's score
Gil Cates's *A Midsummer Night's Rave* (2001)	transposes the action to a drug- and flirt-filled rave party
Tommy O'Haver's *Get Over It* (2001)	built around a musical production of *A Midsummer Night's Dream*

The Darker Side of Magic and Eroticism

Recent adaptations have explored the darker side of *A Midsummer Night's Dream*'s magic and eroticism, the threatening, nightmarish, or dangerously seductive qualities of the fairy world. This element is not entirely new—Reinhardt and Dieterle's 1935 film features an intimidating Oberon dressed in black and emphasizes the unsettling quality of Bottom's transformation until a maternal Titania appears to comfort him. But the potential for tragedy has become more pronounced in many contemporary adaptations. Noble's 1996 film also treats Oberon as a frightening father figure and periodically reminds us how disturbing the play is for the film's child protagonist; John Canemaker's *Bottom's Dream* treats Bottom as a child terrorized by magical phantasmagoria as he metamorphoses into an ass. Hoffman's 1999 film takes the novel approach of sympathetically portraying Bottom as a romantic dreamer denigrated by his shrewish wife. His life is temporarily redeemed by a brief affair with Titania, who is presented as a gauzy sexual fantasy. But she has a troubling side—this Titania won't let Bottom leave the wood (she ensnares him with vines and bridles his tongue), and among the creatures in her bower is a Medusa. Several feminist critics have complained that Hoffman's adaptation makes powerful women into castraters of men, whereas in Shakespeare's script it is Oberon who is the castrater, punishing Titania for her assertiveness. A crucial allusion to the play in *Dead Poets Society* (1989, directed by Peter Weir) also partakes of this darker quality. Encouraged by a charismatic teacher, Neil Perry, a bright student at a conservative prep school, becomes enchanted with theater and gets the role of Puck in a local production of *A Midsummer Night's Dream*. Though Neil is superb in the performance, his overbearing father disapproves of his activities and the conflict between the two quickly escalates into disaster. The allusion to *Midsummer* functions, among other things, to suggest the seductive quality of theatrical "magic" and its potential for both charm and tragedy.

Midsummer CHARACTERS IN POP CULTURE

Over time, a handful of characters from *A Midsummer Night's Dream* have taken on lives of their own in popular culture. Puck, for example, has become a icon for mocking chicanery, identified with his most famous line, "Lord, what fools these mortals be." For many years he and his motto were featured on the banner of Sunday comics in England and the United States. A statue of Puck on the grounds of the Folger Shakespeare Library in Washington, DC faces the Congress Building and Supreme Court and offers sardonic commentary on their political proceedings. Given his reputation, it is appropriate that Puck was played by the bumbling cartoon character Mr. Magoo in "A Midsummer Night's Dream," a 1965 installment of the *Mr. Magoo* animated series. Most recently, Puck has appeared as a sinister stealer of souls in the comic book series *Aria: The Soul Market* (2001). Along with Puck, Titania and Oberon have served as characters in a number of fantasy novels and stories, including most notably L. Sprague de Camp and Fletcher Pratt's *Land of Unreason* (1942), Poul Anderson's *A Midsummer Tempest* (1974), Botho Strauss's *The Park* (1985), Raymond E. Feist's *Fairy Tale* (1988), Gary Kilworth's *A Midsummer's Nightmare* (1996), and Terry Pratchett's *Lords and Ladies* (1996). (Though Roger Zelazny's ten-book Amber fantasy series stars a king named Oberon, he bears no resemblance to Shakespeare's character beyond the name.) Bottom too has been the protagonist of separate tales. Robert Watson's whimsical novel *Whilom* (1990) offers a comic retelling of Shakespeare's narrative, with Bottom as its hapless hero, and animator John Canemaker's short *Bottom's Dream* (1983) portrays Bottom's transformation into a beast as a hallucinatory nightmare, using a dazzling range of animation techniques in the process. Perhaps prompted by the fact that *Midsummer* is one of the few narratives original with Shakespeare, several fantasy works imagine an encounter between Shakespeare and characters from the fairy world. Neil Gaiman's award-winning "A Midsummer Night's Dream" (1995), from his *Sandman* comic book series, imagines Titania, Oberon, Puck and their fairy bands in attendance at Shakespeare and company's travelling production of *Midsummer*. Titania becomes enchanted with Shakespeare's son Hamnet, and Shakespeare, too distracted with details of the performance, fails to notice that she has spirited Hamnet away until it is too late. In Sarah Hoyt's fantasy trilogy, *Ill Met by Moonlight* (2001), *All Night Awake* (2002), and *Any Man So Daring* (2003), Shakespeare has repeated encounters with a fairy prince named Quicksilver, the son of Titania and Oberon who bears a striking resemblance to Puck in magical powers and temperament. Each of these adventures draws upon motifs from *A Midsummer Night's Dream* (and other Shakespeare plays). Hoyt's clever implication is that Shakespeare's contact with the fairy world ultimately provided him the source of his fantastical play.

PARODIES

Perhaps because the play includes its own self-parody, *A Midsummer Night's Dream* has not been an especially favorite target for popular parody. Nonetheless, a smattering of examples do exist, most for the stage and many of them involving the tried-and-true formula of a Shakespearean performance gone awry. *Shakespeare for Fun and Profit (or it sure beats farming)* (1977), a Canadian farce by Paul Thompson, John Gray, and the Theatre Passe Muraille, chronicles the saga of Ontario yokels to put on a performance of Shakespeare's play, along the way offering gentle satire of rural Canadian culture and the Canadian Stratford phenomenon. Two of the more interesting Shakespearean spoofs come from down under. *Revenge of the Amazons* (1989), a comedy by New Zealander Jean Betts, reimagines Shakespeare's narrative from a feminist perspective, with Titania drugging Oberon and placing him in the company of a women's theater troupe. The farce *The Popular Mechanicals* (1987) by Sydney's Belvoir Street Theatre Troupe fleshes out the rehearsal and performance scenes from *Midsummer* with song, clowning, slapstick, bawdry, and puppetry to one-up Shakespeare's own theatrical parody. Geoffrey Rush, the renowned Australian actor, contributed to the script and directed the first production. This pantomime-style comedy was sufficiently popular to spawn a sequel, *The Popular Mechanicals 2* (aka *Pop Mex 2*), in 1992, in which the troupe takes on figures from the Elizabethan court as well as Shakespeare's characters. One of the more remarkable conjunctions of *Midsummer* and pop culture can be found in a 1964 special by the Beatles for British TV. In addition to singing a few songs, the group performs the Mechanicals' play in its entirety and in full costume, with Paul as Pyramus, John as Thisbe, George as Moonshine, and Ringo as Snug. Besides being surprisingly entertaining, the rough-and-ready performance reveals otherwise unexpected kinships between Shakespeare's play-within-the-play, with its goofy wordplay, whimsical, knowing humor, working-class spirit, and surrealistic quality, and the music of the Beatles' psychedelic period.

CROSS-CULTURAL ADAPTATIONS

Though *A Midsummer Night's Dream* is more firmly rooted in British culture than Shakespeare's other comedies (this despite its superficial Athenian setting), the play has become increasingly amenable to cross-cultural adaptations. The film *Un Poco Loco* (1997, directed by Deborah Koons) freely adapts motifs from *Midsummer* to the Anglo-Spanish culture of California, with a magic fungus substituting for Shakespeare's love-in-idleness potion. Likewise, Wole Soyinka's first play, *A Dream of the Forests* (1963), transposes motifs from Shakespeare's play to Yoruban culture in order to criticize African politics. Arjun Raina's *The Magic Hour* (2002) combines scenes of Shakespeare with Raina's own approach to Kathakali dance; appropriately enough for an Indian adaptation, one of the scenes involves Oberon and Titania's fight over the Indian boy. Adaptations for Indian audiences (by Habib Tanvir in 2002) and Egyptian audiences (by Khalid Galal in 2003) indicate the play's growing global reach. Kalyan Ray's postmodern novel *Eastwords* (2005) features a

Puck, Titania, and Oberon (among other Shakespearean characters) who become intertwined with Indian mythological figures as the narrative progresses. Even so, it may be too easy to overestimate the ease with which Shakespeare crosses cultural borders. Tom Weidlinger's documentary *A Dream in Hanoi* (2002) details the attempt of two theater troupes, one American, the other Vietnamese, to mount a joint stage production of *A Midsummer Night's Dream* in Hanoi. Though the film ends in triumph, Weidlinger suggests the enormous gulf that exists between the two cultures involved, a gulf that is complicated, not bridged, by *A Midsummer Night's Dream*. A fascinating and at times painful film to watch, *A Dream in Hanoi* reminds us once again of the extraordinary challenge of adapting Shakespeare's plays to new eras and cultures, but also of its necessity.

Dramatis Personae

THE COURT
Theseus: Duke of Athens
Hippolyta: Queen of the Amazons, betrothed to Theseus
Philostrate: the Master of the Revels to Theseus
Egeus: father to Hermia

THE LOVERS
Hermia: daughter of Egeus, in love with Lysander
Lysander: loved by Hermia
Helena: in love with Demetrius
Demetrius: in love with Hermia and favored by Egeus

THE FAIRIES
Oberon: King of the Fairies
Titania: Queen of the Fairies
Robin Goodfellow: a puck

Peaseblossom
Cobweb   } Titania's attendant fairies
Mote
Mustardseed

THE MECHANICALS   **IN *PYRAMUS & THISBE* AS:**
Peter Quince: a carpenter   Prologue
Nick Bottom: a weaver   Pyramus
Francis Flute: a bellows-mender   Thisbe
Tom Snout: a tinker   Wall
Snug: a joiner   Lion
Robin Starveling: a tailor   Moonshine

Lords and attendants of the court and other attendant fairies

[A Midsummer Night's Dream

Act 1

Location: Theseus's court in Athens. Although the location is noted as "Theseus's court," this scene has been staged in a Greek-style palace, an executive office, an outdoor garden setting, and private apartments within an English-style estate. The common ground seems to be that the setting conveys a sense of elegance and aristocracy.

Scene: Michael Hoffman sets his 1999 film on an estate in the nineteenth century and, with a preface projected on to the screen, he explains to the audience that the phonograph and the bicycle, images that will recur throughout the film, have just been invented.

4: **lingers to:** frustrates by delaying

5: **stepdame:** a stepmother who, because of her position in the family, keeps a young heir from his inheritance
5: **dowager:** a widow who might use up her dead husband's wealth before the heir can inherit.

6: **withering out:** using up

7: **steep:** be immersed, as in a deep slumber

10: **new bent:** an arrow freshly made, just drawn, and poised to fly—like Cupid's arrow.

11: **solemnities:** (marriage) ceremony

16: **I wooed thee with my sword:** According to the source stories, Thomas North's 1579 translation of Plutarch's *Lives of the Noble Grecians and Romans*, Chaucer's *Knight's Tale*, and Ovid's *Metamorphoses*, Theseus defeated and captured Hippolyta in his military conquest of the Amazons.

19: **triumph:** public festivities

tracks 2-4

20–64:
Paul Shelley as Theseus, Amanda Root as Hermia
David Timson as Egeus, Jack Ellis as Theseus, Cathy Sara as Hermia

Act 1, Scene 1]

Enter THESEUS, HIPPOLYTA,
PHILOSTRATE, and Attendants

THESEUS
    Now, fair Hippolyta, our nuptial hour
    Draws on apace; four happy days bring in
    Another moon. But, O, methinks, how slow
    This old moon wanes! She lingers to my desires,
    Like to a stepdame or a dowager   5
    Long withering out a young man's revenue.

HIPPOLYTA
    Four days will quickly steep themselves in night;
    Four nights will quickly dream away the time;
    And then the moon, like to a silver bow
    New bent in heaven, shall behold the night   10
    Of our solemnities.

THESEUS
              Go, Philostrate,
    Stir up the Athenian youth to merriments;
    Awake the pert and nimble spirit of mirth;
    Turn melancholy forth to funerals;
    The pale companion is not for our pomp.   15
                       Exit PHILOSTRATE

    Hippolyta, I wooed thee with my sword
    And won thy love doing thee injuries;
    But I will wed thee in another key,
    With pomp, with triumph, and with reveling.
        Enter EGEUS, HERMIA, LYSANDER, and DEMETRIUS

EGEUS
    Full of vexation come I, with complaint   20
    Against my child, my daughter Hermia,

tracks 2-4

20–64:
Paul Shelley as Theseus, Amanda Root as Hermia
David Timson as Egeus, Jack Ellis as Theseus, Cathy Sara as Hermia

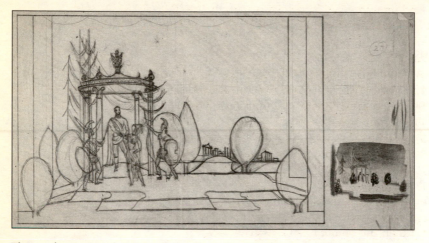

Theseus's courtyard. Set rendering from the March 23, 1954 staging at the Shakespeare Memorial Theatre (Stratford-upon-Avon, England) directed by George Devine with sets and costumes by Margaret Harris

Rare Book and Special Collections Library, University of Illinois at Urbana-Champaign

29: **feigning voice:** deceitful, veiled, singing softly
31: **gawds, conceits:** trinkets and clever gifts
32: **knacks:** small toys or knickknacks
32: **nosegays, sweetmeats:** small bouquets and candy
33: **prevailment:** persuasion
33: **unhardened youth:** an innocent and inexperienced young person
34: **filched:** stolen
37: **be it so:** if
39: **ancient privilege of Athens:** Egeus is referring to an ancient Roman rule called *patria potestas*, where fathers have ultimate power and authority over their daughters until they are married. If they disobey, they can be put to death. This is sometimes referred to as bridling.
43: **immediately:** without intervention
52: **kind:** respect
52: **voice:** approval

Stand forth Demetrius. My noble lord,
This man hath my consent to marry her.
Stand forth, Lysander. And my gracious duke,
This man hath bewitched the bosom of my child;   25
That, thou, Lysander, thou hast given her rhymes
And interchanged love tokens with my child.
Thou hast by moonlight at her window sung,
With feigning voice verses of feigning love,
And stolen the impression of her fantasy   30
With bracelets of thy hair, rings, gawds, conceits,
Knacks, trifles, nosegays, sweetmeats, messengers
Of strong prevailment in unhardened youth.
With cunning hast thou filched my daughter's heart,
Turned her obedience, which is due to me,   35
To stubborn harshness. And, my gracious duke,
Be it so she will not here before your grace
Consent to marry with Demetrius,
I beg the ancient privilege of Athens.
As she is mine, I may dispose of her,   40
Which shall be either to this gentleman
Or to her death, according to our law
Immediately provided in that case.

THESEUS
What say you, Hermia? Be advised fair maid.
To you your father should be as a god;   45
One that composed your beauties, yea, and one
To whom you are but as a form in wax
By him imprinted and within his power
To leave his figure or disfigure it.
Demetrius is a worthy gentleman.   50

HERMIA
So is Lysander.

THESEUS
                    In himself he is;
But in this kind, wanting your father's voice,
The other must be held the worthier.

20–64:
Paul Shelley as Theseus, Amanda Root as Hermia
David Timson as Egeus, Jack Ellis as Theseus, Cathy Sara as Hermia

Line 56: "I do entreat your grace to pardon me": Paris Remillard as Lysander, Noel True as Hermia, Paul Whitthorne as Demetrius (background), Mark H. Dold as Theseus, and Edward Gero as Egeus in the Shakespeare Theatre Company's 2003–04 production directed by Mark Lamos

Photo: Richard Termine

58: **concern:** suit or befit
63: **die the death:** be executed
63: **abjure:** swear to give up
66: **blood:** passion
68: **livery:** clothing of a monk or a nun, usually called a habit
69: **for aye:** forever
69: **mewed:** caged or locked in
72: **blood:** passions
73: **maidenly pilgrimage:** to live as a virgin
74: **earthlier happy:** happier on earth
74: **rose distilled:** (roses were distilled to make perfume)
76: **in single blessedness:** celibate
78: **virgin patent:** right to remain a virgin
79: **unwishèd:** unwanted
82: **sealing day:** day of contract (seal)

HERMIA

    I would my father looked but with my eyes.

THESEUS

    Rather your eyes must with his judgment look.   55

HERMIA

    I do entreat your grace to pardon me.
    I know not by what power I am made bold,
    Nor how it may concern my modesty,
    In such a presence here to plead my thoughts;
    But I beseech your grace that I may know   60
    The worst that may befall me in this case,
    If I refuse to wed Demetrius.

THESEUS

    Either to die the death or to abjure
    Forever the society of men.
    Therefore, fair Hermia, question your desires;   65
    Know of your youth, examine well your blood,
    Whether, if you yield not to your father's choice,
    You can endure the livery of a nun,
    For aye to be in a shady cloister mewed,
    To live a barren sister all your life,   70
    Chanting faint hymns to the cold fruitless moon.
    Thrice-blessed they that master so their blood,
    To undergo such a maidenly pilgrimage;
    But earthlier happy is the rose distilled,
    Than that which withering on the virgin thorn   75
    Grows, lives, and dies in single blessedness.

HERMIA

    So will I grow, so live, so die, my lord,
    Ere I will yield my virgin patent up
    Unto his lordship, whose unwishèd yoke
    My soul consents not to give sovereignty.   80

THESEUS

    Take time to pause, and, by the next new moon—
    The sealing day betwixt my love and me,

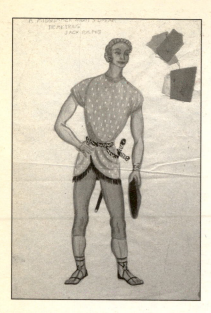

Costume for Demetrius from the 1948 staging directed by George Devine with sets and costumes by Margaret Harris

85: **protest:** vow
86: **austerity:** an ascetic life
88: **crazèd title:** unsound claim
94: **estate:** to relinquish or to give
95: **well derived:** well-descended, of good lineage
96: **well possessed:** wealthy
97: **fairly:** positively, handsomely
98: **vantage:** superiority
101: **prosecute:** pursue
102: **avouch it to his head:** swear it to his face
103: **made love to:** wooed
106: **spotted:** immoral, tainted
106: **inconstant:** fickle
109: **self-affairs:** personal issues
112: **schooling:** advice

For everlasting bond of fellowship—
Upon that day either prepare to wed Demetrius, as he would;
Or on Diana's altar to protest   85
For aye austerity and single life.

DEMETRIUS
Relent, sweet Hermia. And Lysander yield
Thy crazèd title to my certain right.

LYSANDER
You have her father's love, Demetrius;
Let me have Hermia's. Do you marry him.   90

EGEUS
Scornful Lysander! True, he hath my love,
And what is mine my love shall render him.
And she is mine, and all my right of her
I do estate unto Demetrius.

LYSANDER
I am, my lord, as well derived as he,   95
As well possessed; my love is more than his;
My fortunes every way as fairly ranked,
If not with vantage, as Demetrius';
And, which is more than all these boasts can be,
I am beloved of beauteous Hermia.   100
Why should not I then prosecute my right?
Demetrius, I'll avouch it to his head,
Made love to Nedar's daughter, Helena,
And won her soul; and she, sweet lady, dotes,
Devoutly dotes, dotes in idolatry,   105
Upon this spotted and inconstant man.

THESEUS
I must confess that I have heard so much,
And with Demetrius thought to have spoke thereof;
But, being overfull of self-affairs,
My mind did lose it. But, Demetrius, come,   110
And come, Egeus; you shall go with me;
I have some private schooling for you both.

113: **arm:** prepare

116: **extenuate:** lessen

121: **against:** in preparation for

122: **nearly that concerns:** that closely concerns

126: **belike:** probably

127: **beteem:** afford, give

128: **aught:** anything

131: **different in blood:** from a different socioeconomic class or hereditary rank

132: **O cross:** a curse caused by frustration

133: **misgraffèd:** badly matched

133: **respect of years:** i.e., ages

135: **stood upon:** depended on

Costume for Hermia from the 1948 staging directed by George Devine with sets and costumes by Margaret Harris
Rare Book and Special Collections Library, University of Illinois at Urbana-Champaign

For you, fair Hermia, look you arm yourself
To fit your fancies to your father's will;
Or else the law of Athens yields you up—   115
Which by no means we may extenuate—
To death, or to a vow of single life.
Come, my Hippolyta. What cheer, my love?
Demetrius and Egeus, go along.
I must employ you in some business   120
Against our nuptial and confer with you
Of something nearly that concerns yourselves.

EGEUS

With duty and desire we follow you.

Exit all but LYSANDER and HERMIA

LYSANDER

How now, my love! Why is your cheek so pale?
How chance the roses there do fade so fast?   125

HERMIA

Belike for want of rain, which I could well
Beteem them from the tempest of my eyes.

LYSANDER

Ay me! For aught that I could ever read,
Could ever hear by tale or history,
The course of true love never did run smooth;   130
But, either it was different in blood—

HERMIA

O cross! Too high to be enthralled to low.

LYSANDER

Or else misgraffèd in respect of years—

HERMIA

O spite! Too old to be engaged to young.

LYSANDER

Or else it stood upon the choice of friends—   135

137: **a sympathy in choice:** an agreement

141: **collied:** coal-black

142: **in a spleen:** impulsively, swiftly (the spleen was regarded as the source of violent impulses)

143: **ere:** before

145: **so quick:** lively

145: **confusion:** ruin

146: **ever crossed:** forever thwarted

149: **customary:** common

151: **fancy:** sexual attraction

152: **persuasion:** attitude

155: **seven leagues:** about 20 miles or 35 kilometers (a league was intended to represent the distance a person could walk in an hour, about 3 miles or 5 kilometers)

156: **respects:** considers

161: **without:** outside of

163: **observance to a morn of May:** The first of May, or "May Day," was a longtime festival in England. Although it originated in pre-Christian England, Catholicism, far from discouraging it, simply changed it to a celebration of the Blessed Virgin Mary, also called "Our Lady."

165–66: **Cupid's strongest bow . . . golden head:** Cupid carried golden arrows, believed to cause love, and lead arrows, believed to cause dislike

HERMIA
O hell! To choose love by another's eyes.

LYSANDER
Or, if there were a sympathy in choice,
War, death, or sickness did lay siege to it,
Making it momentary as a sound,
Swift as a shadow, short as any dream,   140
Brief as the lightning in the collied night,
That, in a spleen, unfolds both heaven and earth,
And ere a man hath power to say, "Behold!"
The jaws of darkness do devour it up.
So quick bright things come to confusion.   145

HERMIA
If then true lovers have been ever crossed,
It stands as an edict in destiny.
Then let us teach our trial patience
Because it is a customary cross,
As due to love as thoughts and dreams and sighs,   150
Wishes and tears, poor fancy's followers.

LYSANDER
A good persuasion. Therefore, hear me, Hermia.
I have a widow aunt, a dowager
Of great revenue, and she hath no child.
From Athens is her house remote seven leagues,   155
And she respects me as her only son.
There, gentle Hermia, may I marry thee,
And to that place the sharp Athenian law
Cannot pursue us. If thou lovest me then,
Steal forth thy father's house tomorrow night,   160
And in the wood, a league without the town
Where I did meet thee once with Helena
To do observance to a morn of May,
There will I stay for thee.

HERMIA
                    My good Lysander!
I swear to thee, by Cupid's strongest bow,   165

167: **Venus' doves:** (doves pulled Venus's heavenly chariot)

169: **fire which burned the Carthage queen:** funeral pyre on which Dido (the Carthage queen) threw herself when her lover, Aeneas, deserts her

170: **false Trojan:** unfaithful Trojan, i.e., Aeneas

173: **appointed:** met with

tracks 5-7

177–203:
Saskia Wickham as Helena, Amanda Root as Hermia
Emily Raymond as Helena, Cathy Sara as Hermia

177: **fair:** refers to Helena's blonde (Petrarchan) beauty, then the standard for beauty in England

178: **your fair:** i.e., your fair beauty (in this reference to Hermia, "fair" means "handsome"; Hermia is of dark complexion)

178: **happy fair:** i.e., you lucky (happy) fair (beauty)

179: **lodestars:** the stars that guide (as in a compass)

179: **sweet air:** melody

180: **tuneable:** melodious

182: **favor:** looks, appearances

186: **Demetrius being bated:** excluding Demetrius (bated = exempt)

187: **translated:** changed

189: **the motion of Demetrius' heart:** i.e., Demetrius's desire

By his best arrow with the golden head,
By the simplicity of Venus' doves,
By that which knitteth souls and prospers loves,
And by that fire which burned the Carthage queen,
When the false Trojan under sail was seen,   170
By all the vows that ever men have broke,
In number more than ever women spoke,
In that same place thou hast appointed me,
Tomorrow truly will I meet with thee.

LYSANDER
Keep promise, love. Look, here comes Helena.   175
Enter HELENA

HERMIA
God speed fair Helena! Whither away?

HELENA
Call you me fair? That fair again unsay.
Demetrius loves your fair. O happy fair!
Your eyes are lodestars and your tongue's sweet air
More tuneable than lark to shepherd's ear,   180
When wheat is green, when hawthorn buds appear.
Sickness is catching. O, were favor so,
Yours would I catch, fair Hermia, ere I go;
My ear should catch your voice, my eye your eye,
My tongue should catch your tongue's sweet melody.   185
Were the world mine, Demetrius being bated,
The rest I'd give to be to you translated.
O, teach me how you look, and with what art
You sway the motion of Demetrius' heart.

HERMIA
I frown upon him, yet he loves me still.   190

HELENA
O that your frowns would teach my smiles such skill!

HERMIA
I give him curses, yet he gives me love.

177–203:
Saskia Wickham as Helena, Amanda Root as Hermia
Emily Raymond as Helena, Cathy Sara as Hermia

197: would: if only

Lines 198–199: "Take comfort. He no more shall see my face; / Lysander and myself will fly this place": Paris Remillard as Lysander, Kate Nowlin as Helena, and Noel True as Hermia in the Shakespeare Theatre Company's 2003–04 production directed by Mark Lamos
Photo: Richard Termine

202: graces: charms
202: my love: i.e., Lysander
205: Phoebe: referring to Diana, the goddess of the moon
206: visage in the watery glass: reflection in a body of water (e.g., a lake or pond)
207: liquid pearl: i.e., dew
208: still: always
211: faint: pale
211: wont: usually
215: stranger companies: the company of strangers

HELENA
O that my prayers could such affection move!

HERMIA
The more I hate, the more he follows me.

HELENA
The more I love, the more he hateth me.   195

HERMIA
His folly, Helena, is no fault of mine.

HELENA
None but your beauty. Would that fault were mine!

HERMIA
Take comfort. He no more shall see my face;
Lysander and myself will fly this place.
Before the time I did Lysander see,   200
Seemed Athens as a paradise to me.
O, then, what graces in my love do dwell,
That he hath turned a heaven unto a hell!

LYSANDER
Helen, to you our minds we will unfold.
Tomorrow night, when Phoebe doth behold   205
Her silver visage in the watery glass,
Decking with liquid pearl the bladed grass,
A time that lovers' flights doth still conceal,
Through Athens' gates have we devised to steal.

HERMIA
And in the wood, where often you and I   210
Upon faint primrose-beds were wont to lie,
Emptying our bosoms of their counsel sweet,
There my Lysander and myself shall meet;
And thence from Athens turn away our eyes,
To seek new friends and stranger companies.   215
Farewell, sweet playfellow. Pray thou for us;
And good luck grant thee thy Demetrius!
Keep word, Lysander. We must starve our sight
From lovers' food till morrow deep midnight.

Line 222: "How happy some o'er other some can be!": Jean Muir as Helena
in Dieterle/Reinhardt's 1935 production

Courtesy: Douglas Lanier

222: **some o'er other some:** some (people) in comparison to some others
(Helena means Hermia and Lysander compared to Demetrius and herself)
228: **holding no quantity:** shapeless, formless
229: **transpose:** change
230: **Love looks . . . with the mind:** Love is a feeling that one senses rather than
a result of reason
232: **nor hath Love's . . . judgment taste:** i.e., people in love have no judgment
233: **figure:** mean, signify
233: **unheedy:** headstrong, heedless
236: **waggish:** playful
236: **game:** sport
238: **eyne:** eyes
245: **dear:** 1) worthwhile   2) costly

Scene: Peter Brook's 1970 forest was anything but magical. In fact, it did not
resemble a forest at all. The lovers were instead tangled in fishing lines hung from a
catwalk. The stage became a gauntlet of sorts for the lovers to avoid, run from,
escape as best they could, lending the scene a sinister and intimidating aspect.

LYSANDER
  I will, my Hermia.

                                                    Exit HERMIA
                    Helena, *adieu*.   220
  As you on him, Demetrius dote on you!

                                                    Exit LYSANDER

HELENA
  How happy some o'er other some can be!
  Through Athens I am thought as fair as she.
  But what of that? Demetrius thinks not so;
  He will not know what all but he do know.   225
  And as he errs, doting on Hermia's eyes,
  So I, admiring of his qualities.
  Things base and vile, holding no quantity,
  Love can transpose to form and dignity.
  Love looks not with the eyes, but with the mind;   230
  And therefore is winged Cupid painted blind.
  Nor hath Love's mind of any judgment taste;
  Wings and no eyes figure unheedy haste.
  And therefore is love said to be a child,
  Because in choice he is so oft beguiled.   235
  As waggish boys in game themselves forswear,
  So the boy Love is perjured everywhere.
  For ere Demetrius looked on Hermia's eyne,
  He hailed down oaths that he was only mine;
  And when this hail some heat from Hermia felt,   240
  So he dissolved, and showers of oaths did melt.
  I will go tell him of fair Hermia's flight.
  Then to the wood will he tomorrow night
  Pursue her; and for this intelligence,
  If I have thanks, it is a dear expense.   245
  But herein mean I to enrich my pain,
  To have his sight thither and back again.

                                                    Exit

Location: Often staged outside of the palace and the forest, in a village square. Each of the six characters' names represent the respective trade or craft involved: Quince, or "quoin," was a wedge used by carpenters; Snug refers to well-made wooden furniture; Bottom, besides "bottom" connoting "ass," was also a piece of wood that wool or thread was wound around; Flute is in reference to a broken or worn-out bellows, which would whistle through holes like a flute when it was pumped; Snout, as a tinker, would repair, among other things, teapots and their broken spouts (or snouts); Starveling refers to his economic state: since most women and girls could stitch and sew, tailors made little money off their trade, and for that reason, they had little to spend on food and were dependent upon the charity of their customers.

2: **generally:** Bottom misspeaks frequently; here he means to say "individually"

3: **scrip:** script

8: **grow to a point:** reach a conclusion

9–53:
Richard Cordery as Quince, Roy Hudd as Bottom, Alex Lowe as Flute, Sidney Livingstone as Starveling, John Hollis as Snout
John Moffatt as Quince, Warren Mitchell as Bottom, Peter Kenny as Flute, John Rye as Starveling, Don McCorkindale as Snout

tracks 8-10

9: **Marry:** a mild oath (referring to Mary, the Blessed Virgin)

9–10: **the most lamentable comedy and most cruel death of Pyramus and Thisby:** a parody of the overlong titles of other contemporary plays of the period. Based on a story in Ovid's *Metamorphoses*, it also serves as a partial source for Shakespeare's *Romeo and Juliet*.

10: **Thisby:** Note that "Thisbe" is spelled "Thisby" when the performers are speaking. This reflects their colloquial speech and also serves to differentiate between the original Latin story and their interpretation of it.

12–13: **spread yourselves:** stand around a central figure

Act 1, Scene 2]

Enter QUINCE, SNUG, BOTTOM, FLUTE,
SNOUT, and STARVELING

QUINCE
Is all our company here?

BOTTOM
You were best to call them generally, man by man, according to
the scrip.

QUINCE
Here is the scroll of every man's name which is thought fit,
through all Athens, to play in our interlude before the duke and   5
the duchess, on his wedding day at night.

BOTTOM
First, good Peter Quince, say what the play treats on, then read
the names of the actors, and so grow to a point.

QUINCE
Marry, our play is, "The most lamentable comedy and most cruel
death of Pyramus and Thisby."   10

BOTTOM
A very good piece of work, I assure you, and a merry. Now, good
Peter Quince, call forth your actors by the scroll. Masters, spread
yourselves.

QUINCE
Answer as I call you. Nick Bottom, the weaver.

BOTTOM
Ready. Name what part I am for, and proceed.   15

tracks 8-10

9–53:

Richard Cordery as Quince, Roy Hudd as Bottom, Alex Lowe as Flute,
Sidney Livingstone as Starveling, John Hollis as Snout
John Moffatt as Quince, Warren Mitchell as Bottom, Peter Kenny as Flute,
John Rye as Starveling, Don McCorkindale as Snout

Scene: Max Reinhardt was compelled by his producer to use popular vaudevillians turned contracted movie stars for this production. With a few exceptions, it proved to be a success. Actors like James Cagney (Bottom) and Mickey Rooney (Puck) delivered Shakespeare's lines in the accents of 1930s New York youth gangsters, to delightful effect. In this first full-length film production, Cagney comes across as an obnoxious know-it-all, and in the "Pyramus and Thisbe" casting scene, he clearly understands this character type well, hamming it up oh so perfectly. In Hoffman's 1999 production set in Tuscany, beautiful women and lusty men cavort while an Italian opera plays loudly. Bottom (played by Kevin Kline) reveals himself as nothing less than a fickle Italian lover, a hen-pecked husband (lending his character some sympathy), and an obstinate and overbearingly bad actor.

20: **condole:** to arouse pity

21: **humor:** desire

22: **'Erc'les:** Hercules, a mythological hero known for his great strength

22: **tear a cat in:** i.e., rant and rave

22: **make all split:** i.e., elicit a strong or violent reaction

27: **Phibbus' car:** the chariot of Phoebus, the sun god

31: **lofty:** important-sounding

32: **vein:** manner of speech or behavior

QUINCE
You, Nick Bottom, are set down for Pyramus.

BOTTOM
What is Pyramus? A lover, or a tyrant?

QUINCE
A lover that kills himself most gallant for love.

BOTTOM
That will ask some tears in the true performing of it. If I do it, let
the audience look to their eyes. I will move storms, I will condole in   20
some measure. To the rest—yet my chief humor is for a tyrant. I
could play 'Erc'les rarely, or a part to tear a cat in, to make all split.
    The raging rocks
    And shivering shocks
    Shall break the locks   25
    Of prison gates;
    And Phibbus' car
    Shall shine from far
    And make and mar
    The foolish Fates.   30
This was lofty! Now name the rest of the players.
This is 'Erc'les' vein, a tyrant's vein; a lover is
more condoling.

QUINCE
Francis Flute, the bellows-mender.

FLUTE
Here, Peter Quince.   35

QUINCE
Flute, you must take Thisby on you.

FLUTE
What is Thisby? A wandering knight?

QUINCE
It is the lady that Pyramus must love.

tracks 8-10

9–53:
Richard Cordery as Quince, Roy Hudd as Bottom, Alex Lowe as Flute,
Sidney Livingstone as Starveling, John Hollis as Snout
John Moffatt as Quince, Warren Mitchell as Bottom, Peter Kenny as Flute,
John Rye as Starveling, Don McCorkindale as Snout

Line 39: "Nay, faith, let me not play a woman; I have a beard coming": John Livingstone
Rolle as Robin Starveling, David Sabin as Nick Bottom, Edward Gero as Peter Quince,
Greg Felden as Francis Flute, Brad Waller as Snug, and Ryan Artzberger as Tom Snout
in the Shakespeare Theatre Company's 2003–04 production directed by Mark Lamos
Photo: Richard Termine

39: **let me not play a woman:** Since women's parts were played by young men and
boys whose voices had not yet deepened, Flute might have conceivably taken this as
a comment on his masculinity. He references his beard, perhaps to point out his
manliness.

40: **that's all one:** i.e., it doesn't matter

40: **play it in a mask:** Quince informs Flute that he can wear a mask to hide
his beard

40–41: **speak as small as you will:** Quince suggests that Flute speak in as high
a pitch as he is able

42: **an:** if

43: **monstrous:** exceptionally

53: **fitted:** well-cast

FLUTE

Nay, faith, let me not play a woman; I have a beard coming.

QUINCE

That's all one. You shall play it in a mask, and you may speak as   40
small as you will.

BOTTOM

An I may hide my face, let me play Thisby too, I'll speak in a
monstrous little voice. "Thisne, Thisne!" "Ah, Pyramus, lover
dear! Thy Thisby dear, and lady dear!"

QUINCE

No, no; you must play Pyramus. And, Flute, you Thisby.   45

BOTTOM

Well, proceed.

QUINCE

Robin Starveling, the tailor.

STARVELING

Here, Peter Quince.

QUINCE

Robin Starveling, you must play Thisby's mother. Tom Snout, the
tinker.   50

SNOUT

Here, Peter Quince.

QUINCE

You, Pyramus' father. Myself, Thisby's father. Snug, the joiner,
you, the lion's part. And, I hope, here is a play fitted.

SNUG

Have you the lion's part written? Pray you, if it be, give it me, for
I am slow of study.   55

Costume for Peter Quince from the March 23, 1954 staging at the Shakespeare
Memorial Theatre (Stratford-upon-Avon, England) directed by George Devine
with sets and costumes by Margaret Harris
Rare Book and Special Collections Library, University of Illinois at Urbana-Champaign

56: **extempore:** off the cuff (roar however you like)

65: **aggravate:** a "Bottomism," saying one word when you mean another;
here he means "moderate"

66: **sucking dove:** Bottom combines "sucking lamb" and "sitting dove"

66: **an 'twere:** as if it were

68: **proper:** good-looking

72: **discharge it:** act or play the part

73: **orange-tawny:** yellow

73: **purple-in-grain:** red

73–74: **French-crown-color:** a gold coin

QUINCE
You may do it extempore, for it is nothing but roaring.

BOTTOM
Let me play the lion too. I will roar, that I will do any man's heart good to hear me; I will roar, that I will make the duke say "Let him roar again; let him roar again."

QUINCE
An you should do it too terribly, you would fright the duchess and the   60
ladies that they would shriek, and that were enough to hang us all.

ALL
That would hang us, every mother's son.

BOTTOM
I grant you, friends, if that you should fright the ladies out of their wits, they would have no more discretion but to hang us. But I will aggravate my voice so that I will roar you as gently as any   65
sucking dove; I will roar you an 'twere any nightingale.

QUINCE
You can play no part but Pyramus, for Pyramus is a sweet-faced man, a proper man as one shall see in a summer's day, a most lovely gentlemanlike man. Therefore, you must needs play Pyramus.

BOTTOM
Well, I will undertake it. What beard were I best to play it in?   70

QUINCE
Why, what you will.

BOTTOM
I will discharge it in either your straw-color beard, your orange-tawny beard, your purple-in-grain beard, or your French-crown-color beard, your perfect yellow.

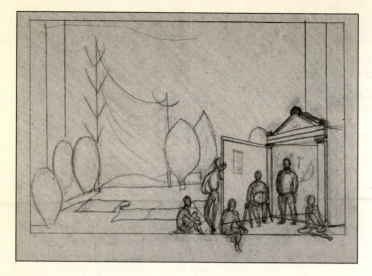

Peter Quince's shop. Set rendering from the March 23, 1954 staging at the
Shakespeare Memorial Theatre (Stratford-upon-Avon, England) directed by
George Devine with sets and costumes by Margaret Harris
Rare Book and Special Collections Library, University of Illinois at Urbana-Champaign

75: some of your French crowns have no hair at all: venereal disease, often called
the "French disease," caused baldness

77: con: memorize

78: without: outside

80: dogged with: bothered by

80: devices: plans (for the play)

81: draw a bill of properties: list the stage props

83: obscenely: Bottom means something else; other editors have suggested "seemly"

84: be perfect: memorize your lines exactly; learn your parts

86: hold or cut bowstrings: i.e., keep your word or be disgraced

QUINCE

   Some of your French crowns have no hair at all, and then you will   75
play bare-faced. But, masters, here are your parts. And I am to
entreat you, request you, and desire you to con them by tomorrow
night and meet me in the palace wood, a mile without the town,
by moonlight. There will we rehearse, for if we meet in the city,
we shall be dogged with company, and our devices known. In the   80
meantime, I will draw a bill of properties such as our play wants.
I pray you, fail me not.

BOTTOM

   We will meet, and there we may rehearse most obscenely and
courageously. Take pains; be perfect. *Adieu.*

QUINCE

   At the duke's oak we meet.   85

BOTTOM

   Enough. Hold or cut bowstrings.

                                                         Exit All

[A Midsummer Night's Dream

Act 2

Location: The forest outside of, and surrounding Athens. This is a magical place, full of fairies and at least one mischievous puck, called Robin Goodfellow. A puck was a common figure in English folklore and was believed to help industrious housemaids if he was treated well—but he was fickle and could also play tricks on them. After introducing Puck talking to a fairy, the scene moves to the argument between the King and Queen of the fairies, Oberon and Titania.

Scene: Puck, that hobgoblin of housewives, is introduced in Act 2, Scene 1. At the time of Reinhardt's filming, Mickey Rooney was only 14, and looked even younger. He plays Puck with a childlike glee, his high-pitched and always laughing voice invading the moon-bright forest. It works up to a point, but by the time Titania and Bottom enter their love-bower, Puck is more annoying than mischievous. In his 1999 film, Hoffman created the opposite effect with Stanley Tucci, an older and more experienced Puck. Puck changes size, appears and disappears at will, ponders questions posed to him by Oberon, and is sadly sage-like when he pronounces the foolishness of mortals. The longer Tucci is on the screen, the more intriguing his character becomes. He is wise for a hobgoblin, much wiser than his "master," the sexy but somewhat uninspired and seemingly bored Oberon.

4: **pale:** a fence
7: **moon's sphere:** According to Ptolemy, the planets, stars, and the sun revolved around a spherical Earth in a perfectly circular path.
9: **dew:** moisten with dew
9: **orbs:** fairy rings, circles of dark grass within which fairies danced and lived
10: **pensioners:** royal bodyguards
12: **favors:** tokens of love
13: **savors:** scents
16: **lob:** country bumpkins
17: **anon:** very soon
20: **passing:** extremely
20: **fell:** terrible, dangerous
20: **wrath:** very angry
23: **changeling:** a stolen child (It was commonly believed that fairies had the power to exchange an unhealthy fairy child for a healthy human baby. The exchanged children were then referred to as changelings.)
25: **trace:** wander

Act 2, Scene 1]

PUCK
How now, spirit! Whither wander you?

Fairy
>Over hill, over dale,
>Through bush, through brier,
>Over park, over pale,
>Through flood, through fire,   5
>I do wander everywhere,
>Swifter than the moon's sphere;
>And I serve the fairy queen,
>To dew her orbs upon the green.
>The cowslips tall her pensioners be.   10
>In their gold coats spots you see;
>Those be rubies, fairy favors,
>In those freckles live their savors.
>I must go seek some dewdrops here
>And hang a pearl in every cowslip's ear.   15

Farewell, thou lob of spirits; I'll be gone.
Our queen and all our elves come here anon.

PUCK
The king doth keep his revels here tonight.
Take heed the queen come not within his sight;
For Oberon is passing fell and wrath   20
Because that she as her attendant hath
A lovely boy stolen from an Indian king;
She never had so sweet a changeling.
And jealous Oberon would have the child
Knight of his train, to trace the forests wild;   25

26: **perforce:** by force

26: **withholds:** keeps

29: **spangled starlight sheen:** light of the shining stars

30: **square:** argue

33: **shrewd:** mischievous, impish

36: **skim milk:** steal the cream from the milk (cream rises to the top)

36: **quern:** a hand mill

37: **bootless . . . housewife churn:** i.e., the housewife churns uselessly, producing no butter (bootless = useless)

38: **make . . . no barm:** i.e., makes flat ale (barm = froth on ale)

42: **aright:** correctly

45: **beguile:** trick

47: **gossip:** an old housewife

48: **roasted crab:** drink made from roasted apples and ale

50: **withered dewlap:** the wrinkled skin on an aged person's neck

51: **saddest:** most serious

54: **"Tailor":** a cry of distress (Tailors would often sit cross-legged on the floor to work, and the housewife's cry might be a reference to finding herself in that position.)

55: **quire:** choir

56: **waxen:** increase

56: **neeze:** sneeze

58: **room:** make room

Beatrice Ferrar as Puck and Walter Hampden as Oberon in a 1905 production
Courtesy: Harry Rusche

But she perforce withholds the lovèd boy,
Crowns him with flowers, and makes him all her joy.
And now they never meet in grove or green,
By fountain clear, or spangled starlight sheen,
But they do square, that all their elves for fear   30
Creep into acorn-cups and hide them there.

Fairy
Either I mistake your shape and making quite,
Or else you are that shrewd and knavish sprite
Called Robin Goodfellow. Are not you he
That frights the maidens of the villagery,   35
Skim milk and sometimes labor in the quern,
And bootless make the breathless housewife churn,
And sometime make the drink to bear no barm,
Mislead night-wanderers, laughing at their harm?
Those that "Hobgoblin" call you, and "sweet Puck,"   40
You do their work, and they shall have good luck.
Are not you he?

PUCK
                    Thou speak'st aright;
I am that merry wanderer of the night.
I jest to Oberon and make him smile
When I a fat and bean-fed horse beguile,   45
Neighing in likeness of a filly foal.
And sometime lurk I in a gossip's bowl,
In very likeness of a roasted crab,
And when she drinks, against her lips I bob
And on her withered dewlap pour the ale.   50
The wisest aunt, telling the saddest tale,
Sometime for three-foot stool mistaketh me;
Then slip I from her bum, down topples she,
And "Tailor" cries, and falls into a cough;
And then the whole quire hold their hips and laugh,   55
And waxen in their mirth and neeze and swear
A merrier hour was never wasted there.
But, room, fairy! Here comes Oberon.

Scene: Reinhardt's beautifully crafted black-and-white film accentuates the effect of a star-filled night as Titania and her fairies enter the scene on falling stars and black Oberon rides the night as though it were a black horse. It is one of the most effective filmic moments in the history of *Dream* on film, especially impressive since it was made in the earliest years of cinema.

Scene: Since Hoffman has set the scene in the late nineteenth century, the fairies (especially Puck) are shown to be as intrigued by the inventions of the humans as the humans are by their fairy power. In contrast to earlier productions where humans are completely at the mercy of fairies, Hoffman depicts them as primitive creatures, totally mystified by human inventions like bicycles and phonographs (called victrolas).

tracks 11-13

60–87:
David Harewood as Oberon, Adjoa Andoh as Titania
Michael Maloney as Oberon, Sarah Woodward as Titania

62: **forsworn:** formally renounced

63: **rash wanton:** thoughtless and immoral woman (it was considered immoral for a woman to deny her husband anything.)

66, 68: **Corin, Phillida:** common names for shepherds

67: **playing on pipes of corn and versing love:** playing on a reed instrument and reciting love poetry

70: **forsooth:** in truth

71: **buskined:** wearing hunting boots

75: **glance at my credit:** question my reputation or my word

78–80: **From Perigenia . . . and Antiopa:** Perigrina and Aegles were mistresses of Theseus. Ariadne, another mistress, helped Theseus kill the Minotaur and escape from Crete, but Theseus later abandons her. Antiopa was the Queen of Amazons and wife of Theseus. All four women were women were betrayed by Theseus, and Oberon charges Titania with having helped him. (Shakespeare's source for Theseus and Hippolyta is Plutarch's *Life of Theseus*.)

Fairy
　　And here my mistress. Would that he were gone!

　　　　　　　Enter separately: OBERON, the king of fairies, with his
　　　　　　　train and TITANIA, the queen of fairies, with hers

OBERON
　　Ill met by moonlight, proud Titania.　　　　　　　　　　　　　　60

TITANIA
　　What, jealous Oberon! Fairies, skip hence.
　　I have forsworn his bed and company.

OBERON
　　Tarry, rash wanton. Am not I thy lord?

TITANIA
　　Then I must be thy lady. But I know
　　When thou hast stolen away from fairyland,　　　　　　　　　　65
　　And in the shape of Corin sat all day,
　　Playing on pipes of corn and versing love
　　To amorous Phillida. Why art thou here,
　　Come from the farthest steppe of India?
　　But that, forsooth, the bouncing Amazon,　　　　　　　　　　　70
　　Your buskined mistress and your warrior love,
　　To Theseus must be wedded, and you come
　　To give their bed joy and prosperity.

OBERON
　　How canst thou thus for shame, Titania,
　　Glance at my credit with Hippolyta,　　　　　　　　　　　　　75
　　Knowing I know thy love to Theseus?
　　Didst thou not lead him through the glimmering night
　　From Perigenia, whom he ravished?
　　And make him with fair Aegles break his faith,
　　With Ariadne and Antiopa?　　　　　　　　　　　　　　　80

tracks 11-13

60–87:
David Harewood as Oberon, Adjoa Andoh as Titania
Michael Maloney as Oberon, Sarah Woodward as Titania

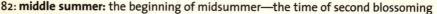

82: **middle summer:** the beginning of midsummer—the time of second blossoming
83: **mead:** meadow
84: **rushy:** fringed with long grasses
85: **margent:** edge, margin
86: **dance our ringlets:** dance in circles (like dancing around a Maypole)
88: **piping:** whistling
90: **contagious:** noxious
91: **pelting:** small or insignificant
92: **continents:** banks
94: **green corn:** unripe grain
95: **ere:** before
95: **attained a beard:** grain that has ripened is said to be "bearded"
97: **murrion:** diseased and dead
98: **nine men's morris:** a popular game played in the countryside; its playing field was cut into the turf
99: **quaint:** intricate, elaborate
99: **wanton:** lush
101: **want:** are in need of
104: **washes all the air:** rains a misty drizzle
105: **that:** so that
105: **rheumatic diseases:** respiratory ailments such as colds
106: **distemperature:** damp weather
109: **Hiems:** the winter god
110: **chaplet:** wreath
112: **childing:** fruitful, pregnant
113: **wonted liveries:** usual clothing
113: **mazèd:** bewildered
114: **increase:** crop yields
116: **debate:** argument
117: **original:** origins

TITANIA
    These are the forgeries of jealousy.
    And never, since the middle summer's spring,
    Met we on hill, in dale, forest or mead,
    By paved fountain or by rushy brook,
    Or in the beachèd margent of the sea,   85
    To dance our ringlets to the whistling wind,
    But with thy brawls thou hast disturbed our sport.
    Therefore the winds, piping to us in vain,
    As in revenge, have sucked up from the sea
    Contagious fogs, which falling in the land,   90
    Have every pelting river made so proud
    That they have overborne their continents.
    The ox hath therefore stretched his yoke in vain,
    The ploughman lost his sweat, and the green corn
    Hath rotted ere his youth attained a beard.   95
    The fold stands empty in the drownèd field,
    And crows are fatted with the murrion flock.
    The nine men's morris is filled up with mud,
    And the quaint mazes in the wanton green,
    For lack of tread are undistinguishable.   100
    The human mortals want their winter here;
    No night is now with hymn or carol blest.
    Therefore the moon, the governess of floods,
    Pale in her anger, washes all the air,
    That rheumatic diseases do abound.   105
    And through this distemperature we see
    The seasons alter. Hoary-headed frosts
    Fall in the fresh lap of the crimson rose,
    And on old Hiems' thin and icy crown
    An odorous chaplet of sweet summer buds   110
    Is, as in mockery, set. The spring, the summer,
    The childing autumn, angry winter, change
    Their wonted liveries, and the mazèd world,
    By their increase, now knows not which is which.
    And this same progeny of evils comes   115
    From our debate, from our dissension.
    We are their parents and original.

118: **amend:** heal

121: **henchman:** a personal servant

121: **set you heart at rest:** don't even worry about it

123: **vot'ress:** a woman who has taken a vow to serve

127: **traders on the flood:** merchant ships at sea

129: **wanton:** playful, amorous

130: **swimming:** smooth

140: **round:** circle dance

142: **spare your haunts:** avoid the places you frequent

Line 143: "Give me that boy, and I will go with thee": Kathleen Widdoes as Titania and James Earl Jones as Oberon in the Public Theater's 1961–62 production directed by Joel Friedman
Photo: George E. Joseph

145: **chide:** argue

145: **downright:** outright

OBERON
    Do you amend it then; it lies in you.
    Why should Titania cross her Oberon?
    I do but beg a little changeling boy,   120
    To be my henchman.

TITANIA
                Set your heart at rest.
    The fairyland buys not the child of me.
    His mother was a vot'ress of my order.
    And, in the spicèd Indian air, by night,
    Full often hath she gossiped by my side,   125
    And sat with me on Neptune's yellow sands,
    Marking th'embarkèd traders on the flood,
    When we have laughed to see the sails conceive
    And grow big-bellied with the wanton wind;
    Which she, with pretty and with swimming gait   130
    Following—her womb then rich with my young squire—
    Would imitate and sail upon the land
    To fetch me trifles and return again,
    As from a voyage, rich with merchandise.
    But she, being mortal, of that boy did die;   135
    And for her sake do I rear up her boy,
    And for her sake I will not part with him.

OBERON
    How long within this wood intend you stay?

TITANIA
    Perchance till after Theseus' wedding day.
    If you will patiently dance in our round   140
    And see our moonlight revels, go with us;
    If not, shun me, and I will spare your haunts.

OBERON
    Give me that boy, and I will go with thee.

TITANIA
    Not for thy fairy kingdom. Fairies, away!
    We shall chide downright, if I longer stay.   145

                      Exit TITANIA with her train

146: **from:** go from
147: **injury:** to insult
151: **harmonious breath:** sweet songs
153: **spheres:** orbits (see note 2.1.7)

Lines 155-157: "That very time I saw, but thou couldst not, / Flying between the cold moon and the earth, / Cupid all armed": Carl Lumbly as Oberon and Geoffrey Owens as Puck in the Public Theater's 1987–88 production directed by A. J. Antoon

Photo: George E. Joseph

157: **all:** fully
158: **vestal:** chaste woman, i.e., vestal virgin
159: **love-shaft:** golden arrow
160: **as:** as though
162: **watery moon:** alluding to the moon's control of the tides
164: **fancy-free:** free of fancies (love's spells)
168: **love-in-idleness:** pansy, heartsease
171: **or man or woman:** either man or woman
174: **leviathan:** a whale
174: **league:** approximately 3 miles or 5 kilometers (see note 1.1.155)

OBERON

    Well, go thy way. Thou shalt not from this grove
    Till I torment thee for this injury.
    My gentle Puck, come hither. Thou rememb'rest
    Since once I sat upon a promontory,
    And heard a mermaid on a dolphin's back   150
    Uttering such dulcet and harmonious breath
    That the rude sea grew civil at her song,
    And certain stars shot madly from their spheres
    To hear the sea-maid's music.

PUCK

            I remember.

OBERON

    That very time I saw, but thou couldst not,   155
    Flying between the cold moon and the earth,
    Cupid all armed. A certain aim he took
    At a fair vestal thronèd by the west,
    And loosed his love-shaft smartly from his bow,
    As it should pierce a hundred thousand hearts;   160
    But I might see young Cupid's fiery shaft
    Quenched in the chaste beams of the watery moon,
    And the imperial vot'ress passèd on,
    In maiden meditation, fancy-free.
    Yet marked I where the bolt of Cupid fell.   165
    It fell upon a little western flower,
    Before milk-white, now purple with love's wound,
    And maidens call it love-in-idleness.
    Fetch me that flower; the herb I shewed thee once.
    The juice of it on sleeping eyelids laid   170
    Will make or man or woman madly dote
    Upon the next live creature that it sees.
    Fetch me this herb, and be thou here again
    Ere the leviathan can swim a league.

175: girdle: circle

185: render up her page: give up her page (her changeling)

Scene: This scene usually gets mixed reactions—especially from women who see Helena as a pathetic figure chasing a man who does not love her and debasing herself in the process. Yet, in Hoffman's production, Calista Flockhart plays the role with a feistiness that belies her desperation, as she stubbornly pushes her bicycle through the mud and the brambles of the forest. Her portrayal is reminiscent of Olivia De Havilland's fiery interpretation in the much earlier Reinhardt film.

192: wode: insane

195: adamant: stone with magnetic properties

197: leave you: surrender

199: speak you fair: speak to you nicely

Line 199: "Do I entice you? Do I speak you fair?": Richard Gere as Demetrius in the Public Theater's 1974–75 production directed by Edward Berkeley
Photo: George E. Joseph

PUCK
> I'll put a girdle round about the earth   175
> In forty minutes.

> *Exit PUCK*

OBERON
>   Having once this juice,
> I'll watch Titania when she is asleep,
> And drop the liquor of it in her eyes.
> The next thing then she waking looks upon,
> Be it on lion, bear, or wolf, or bull,   180
> On meddling monkey, or on busy ape,
> She shall pursue it with the soul of love.
> And ere I take this charm from off her sight,
> As I can take it with another herb,
> I'll make her render up her page to me.   185
> But who comes here? I am invisible;
> And I will overhear their conference.
> *Enter DEMETRIUS, with HELENA following him*

DEMETRIUS
> I love thee not, therefore pursue me not.
> Where is Lysander and fair Hermia?
> The one I'll slay, the other slayeth me.   190
> Thou told'st me they were stolen unto this wood;
> And here am I, and wode within this wood,
> Because I cannot meet my Hermia.
> Hence, get thee gone, and follow me no more.

HELENA
> You draw me, you hard-hearted adamant;   195
> But yet you draw not iron, for my heart
> Is true as steel. Leave you your power to draw,
> And I shall have no power to follow you.

DEMETRIUS
> Do I entice you? Do I speak you fair?
> Or, rather, do I not in plainest truth   200
> Tell you, I do not, nor I cannot love you?

214: **impeach:** question

218: **counsel:** secrecy, privacy

218: **desert:** deserted

220: **privilege:** protection

224: **for you in my respect:** as far as I'm concerned

227: **brakes:** a thicket or and undergrowth

Costume for Helena from the 1948 staging directed by George Devine with sets and costumes by Margaret Harris
Rare Book and Special Collections Library, University of Illinois at Urbana-Champaign

HELENA

    And even for that do I love you the more.
    I am your spaniel; and, Demetrius,
    The more you beat me, I will fawn on you.
    Use me but as your spaniel, spurn me, strike me,   205
    Neglect me, lose me; only give me leave,
    Unworthy as I am, to follow you.
    What worser place can I beg in your love—
    And yet a place of high respect with me—
    Than to be usèd as you use your dog?   210

DEMETRIUS

    Tempt not too much the hatred of my spirit,
    For I am sick when I do look on thee.

HELENA

    And I am sick when I look not on you.

DEMETRIUS

    You do impeach your modesty too much,
    To leave the city and commit yourself   215
    Into the hands of one that loves you not;
    To trust the opportunity of night
    And the ill counsel of a desert place
    With the rich worth of your virginity.

HELENA

    Your virtue is my privilege. For that   220
    It is not night when I do see your face,
    Therefore I think I am not in the night;
    Nor doth this wood lack worlds of company,
    For you in my respect are all the world.
    Then how can it be said I am alone,   225
    When all the world is here to look on me?

DEMETRIUS

    I'll run from thee and hide me in the brakes,
    And leave thee to the mercy of wild beasts.

231–32: Apollo flies . . . the mild hind: In Greek mythology, Daphne flees from Apollo and is transformed into a laurel tree in order to escape him; here the situation is reversed and Apollo flies from Daphne

232: griffin: a monster with a lion's body but the head and wings of an eagle

232: hind: doe

233: bootless: useless

235: I will not stay thy questions: I won't stay here and talk to you any longer

240: your wrongs do set a scandal on my sex: Here, Helena plays the victim blaming Demetrius for her predicament; because he's not interested in her, she tells him that he has forced her to chase him—upsetting the usual patriarchal system.

246: fly: flee from

Line 247: "Hast thou the flower there? Welcome, wanderer": Puck in Jiri Trnka's 1961 production

Courtesy: Douglas Lanier

HELENA

    The wildest hath not such a heart as you.

    Run when you will, the story shall be changed.   230

    Apollo flies, and Daphne holds the chase;

    The dove pursues the griffin; the mild hind

    Makes speed to catch the tiger; bootless speed,

    When cowardice pursues and valor flies.

DEMETRIUS

    I will not stay thy questions; let me go.   235

    Or, if thou follow me, do not believe

    But I shall do thee mischief in the wood.

HELENA

    Ay, in the temple, in the town, the field,

    You do me mischief. Fie, Demetrius!

    Your wrongs do set a scandal on my sex.   240

    We cannot fight for love, as men may do;

    We should be wooed and were not made to woo.

Exit DEMETRIUS
HELENA follows him

I'll follow thee and make a heaven of hell,

To die upon the hand I love so well.

OBERON becomes visible and watches them leave

OBERON

    Fare thee well, nymph. Ere he do leave this grove,   245

    Thou shalt fly him and he shall seek thy love.

Enter PUCK

Hast thou the flower there? Welcome, wanderer.

PUCK

    Ay, there it is.

tracks 14-16

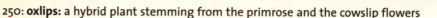

249–267:
Sir John Gielgud as Oberon
Michael Maloney as Oberon

250: **oxlips:** a hybrid plant stemming from the primrose and the cowslip flowers

251: **woodbine:** honeysuckle

252: **muskroses:** very fragrant white roses

252: **eglantine:** a kind of rose

253: **sometime of:** during part of

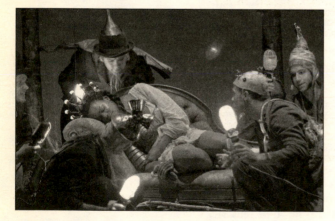

Line 253: "There sleeps Titania sometime of the night": Lisa Tharps as Titania and ensemble members as the Fairies in the Shakespeare Theatre Company's 2003–04 production directed by Mark Lamos
Photo: Richard Termine

255: **throws:** sheds

256: **weed:** garment

257: **streak:** anoint

267: **ere:** before

OBERON
               I pray thee, give it me.
I know a bank where the wild thyme blows,
Where oxlips and the nodding violet grows,   250
Quite overcanopied with luscious woodbine,
With sweet muskroses and with eglantine.
There sleeps Titania sometime of the night,
Lulled in these flowers with dances and delight;
And there the snake throws her enameled skin,   255
Weed wide enough to wrap a fairy in.
And with the juice of this I'll streak her eyes,
And make her full of hateful fantasies.
Take thou some of it, and seek through this grove.
A sweet Athenian lady is in love   260
With a disdainful youth. Anoint his eyes,
But do it when the next thing he espies
May be the lady. Thou shalt know the man
By the Athenian garments he hath on.
Effect it with some care, that he may prove   265
More fond on her than she upon her love.
And look thou meet me ere the first cock crow.

PUCK
Fear not, my lord, your servant shall do so.
                                 Exit both, in different directions

Location: In another part of the forest. Titania and her fairy attendants dance and sing before going to bed.

Scene: In Adrian Noble's 1996 film for the BBC series, the fairies all wear hats with parasols on top, making them bob and sway like mushrooms as they sing back and forth to each other. In stark contrast to Noble, who took his inspiration from Brook's production, Hoffman created a Celtic and gypsy-like illusion with the mead-loving and intoxicated fairies, looking every bit like creatures from a *Star Trek* universe. Titania's attendants are all different, appearing spangled and glittery in all the colors of the rainbow. It fits, especially since it is raining when Helena enters the forest.

Line 1: "Come, now a roundel and a fairy song": Michelle Pfeiffer as Titania with fairy attendants in Michael Hoffman's 1999 production
Courtesy: Douglas Lanier

1: **roundel:** a circular dance
2: **for the third part of a minute:** (indicates how quickly the fairies flit about)
3: **cankers:** caterpillars (called cankerworms)
4: **reremice:** bats
7: **quaint:** small and delicate
8: **offices:** duties
8: **let me rest:** indicating that Titania is reclining
9: **double:** forked
11: **newts:** small water lizards
11: **blind-worms:** small snakes with tiny eyes
13: **Philomel:** the nightingale (in Ovid's *Metamorphoses*, Philomel is turned into a nightingale after she is raped by her sister's husband)

Act 2, Scene 2]

TITANIA
Come, now a roundel and a fairy song;
Then, for the third part of a minute, hence;
Some to kill cankers in the muskrose buds,
Some war with reremice for their leathern wings
To make my small elves coats, and some keep back   5
The clamorous owl that nightly hoots and wonders
At our quaint spirits. Sing me now asleep;
Then to your offices and let me rest.

Fairies sing

FIRST FAIRY
You spotted snakes with double tongue,
Thorny hedgehogs, be not seen;   10
Newts and blind-worms, do no wrong,
Come not near our fairy queen.

Chorus
Philomel, with melody
Sing in our sweet lullaby;
Lulla, lulla, lullaby, lulla, lulla, lullaby.   15
Never harm,
Nor spell nor charm,
Come our lovely lady nigh;
So, good night, with lullaby.

SECOND FAIRY
Weaving spiders, come not here;   20
Hence, you long-legged spinners, hence!
Beetles black, approach not near;
Worm nor snail, do no offense.

Line 24: "Philomel, with melody / Sing in our sweet lullaby": Anita Louise as Titania with fairy attendants in Dieterle/Reinhardt's 1935 production
Courtesy: Douglas Lanier

32: aloof: apart

Scene: With the exception of Brook's and Ciulei's productions, the fairies bring with them an awareness of the magical and pagan essence that lingers in the forest, away from yet part of the human world with which they interact. In Reinhardt's production, Titania resembles the Blue Fairy in Walt Disney's *Pinocchio*, but Oberon is a powerfully dark presence, a presence that overwhelms whatever power the misty Titania might possess. This Oberon (later turned into the equally malicious Auberon in *Dream Country*, volume three of Neil Gaiman's *Sandman* series) is clearly in control, tricking Titania into neglecting the changeling child long enough for him to laughingly snatch the boy away. By contrast, in Hoffman's film, Oberon is no match for Titania; he needs Puck's help to enchant her. Even then, she surrenders more out of bewilderment than weakness.

36: ounce: lynx

37: pard: leopard

42: troth: truthfully

Chorus

      Philomel, with melody
      Sing in our sweet lullaby;   25
      Lulla, lulla, lullaby, lulla, lulla, lullaby.
      Never harm,
      Nor spell nor charm,
      Come our lovely lady nigh;
      So, good night, with lullaby.   30

                           TITANIA sleeps

FIRST FAIRY

  Hence, away! Now all is well.
  One aloof stand sentinel.

                         Exit fairies
                        Enter OBERON

OBERON [*squeezing the nectar on TITANIA's eyelids*]

      What thou seest when thou dost wake,
      Do it for thy true-love take,
      Love and languish for his sake.   35
      Be it ounce, or cat, or bear,
      Pard, or boar with bristled hair,
      In thy eye that shall appear
      When thou wakest, it is thy dear.
      Wake when some vile thing is near.   40

                         Exit OBERON
             Enter LYSANDER and HERMIA

LYSANDER

  Fair love, you faint with wand'ring in the wood;
  And to speak troth, I have forgot our way.
  We'll rest us, Hermia, if you think it good,
  And tarry for the comfort of the day.

HERMIA

  Be it so, Lysander. Find you out a bed,   45
  For I upon this bank will rest my head.

48: troth: faithful vow

Costume for Lysander from the 1948 staging directed by George Devine with sets and costumes by Margaret Harris

Rare Book and Special Collections Library, University of Illinois at Urbana-Champaign

51: sense: true meaning

52: love's conference: an understanding between lovers

58: lying so: i.e., resting in this way

58: lie: deceive (a pun on lying down)

60: beshrew: to curse mildly

63: human: courteous (or humane)

71: with half that wish the wisher's eyes be pressed: I hope that you sleep well

LYSANDER
    One turf shall serve as pillow for us both;
    One heart, one bed, two bosoms and one troth.

HERMIA
    Nay, good Lysander; for my sake, my dear,
    Lie further off yet, do not lie so near.   50

LYSANDER
    O, take the sense, sweet, of my innocence!
    Love takes the meaning in love's conference.
    I mean, that my heart unto yours is knit
    So that but one heart we can make of it;
    Two bosoms interchainèd with an oath;   55
    So then two bosoms and a single troth.
    Then by your side no bedroom me deny;
    For lying so, Hermia, I do not lie.

HERMIA
    Lysander riddles very prettily.
    Now much beshrew my manners and my pride,   60
    If Hermia meant to say Lysander lied.
    But, gentle friend, for love and courtesy,
    Lie further off in human modesty.
    Such separation as may well be said
    Becomes a virtuous bachelor and a maid,   65
    So far be distant; and, good night, sweet friend.
    Thy love ne'er alter till thy sweet life end!

LYSANDER
    Amen, amen, to that fair prayer, say I;
    And then end life when I end loyalty!
    Here is my bed. Sleep give thee all his rest!   70

HERMIA
    With half that wish the wisher's eyes be pressed!

                                            They sleep apart
                                            Enter PUCK

Scene: Puck's mistake—he puts the nectar in the eyes of Lysander instead of Demetrius—is easy to make since the two lovers are so alike, a situation that adds to the humor of the scene. Mickey Rooney's error can be taken for childish impudence and trickery, but Stanley Tucci plays Puck in all seriousness. His mistake is an honest one, and his shrug of "Who knew?" to the exasperated Oberon is a droll acknowledgement of the mischief he has unwittingly caused.

72–89:
Richard McCabe as Puck
Ian Hughes as Puck

Costume for Puck from the 1948 staging directed by George Devine with sets and costumes by Margaret Harris

Rare Book and Special Collections Library, University of Illinois at Urbana-Champaign

74: **approve:** test
77: **weeds:** garments
84: **churl:** rude person
85: **owe:** own
86–87: **let love forbid . . . thy eyelid:** i.e., let thoughts of love keep you awake (forbid sleep his seat)
92: **darkling leave me:** don't leave me alone in the dark
93: **on thy peril:** at your own risk
94: **fond:** doting
95: **my grace:** the favor I receive
96: **lies:** dwells

PUCK
    Through the forest have I gone.
    But Athenian found I none,
    On whose eyes I might approve
    This flower's force in stirring love.   75
    Night and silence—Who is here?
    Weeds of Athens he doth wear.
    This is he, my master said,
    Despisèd the Athenian maid;
    And here the maiden, sleeping sound,   80
    On the dank and dirty ground.
    Pretty soul! She durst not lie
    Near this lack-love, this kill-courtesy.
    Churl, upon thy eyes I throw
    All the power this charm doth owe.   85
                Squeezing nectar on LYSANDER'S eyelids
    When thou wakest, let love forbid
    Sleep his seat on thy eyelid.
    So awake when I am gone,
    For I must now to Oberon.

                              Exit
              Enter DEMETRIUS and HELENA

HELENA
    Stay, though thou kill me, sweet Demetrius.   90

DEMETRIUS
    I charge thee, hence, and do not haunt me thus.

HELENA
    O, wilt thou darkling leave me? Do not so.

DEMETRIUS
    Stay, on thy peril. I alone will go.

                    Exit DEMETRIUS

HELENA
    O, I am out of breath in this fond chase!
    The more my prayer, the lesser is my grace.   95
    Happy is Hermia, wheresoe'er she lies;

102–03: **no marvel . . . my presence thus:** no wonder Demetrius runs away from me as if I were a monster
104: **dissembling glass:** deceitful mirror
105: **compare:** compete
105: **sphery eyne:** shining (as the stars) eyes

Line 109: "And run through fire I will for they sweet sake": Dominic West as Lysander and Calista Flockhart as Helena in Michael Hoffman's 1999 production
Courtesy: Douglas Lanier

110: **transparent:** radiant
110: **art:** skill, power
115: **what though he love your Hermia:** i.e., what of your love for Hermia
120: **change:** exchange
121: **will:** desire (there was a belief prevalent in the Early Modern period that the passions were in constant conflict with the reason)
124: **till now ripe not to reason:** i.e., until now, I wasn't old enough to be rational
125: **touching now the point of human skill:** reaching now the pinnacle of judgment or discernment
126: **marshal:** leader
127: **o'erlook:** read over

For she hath blessèd and attractive eyes.
How came her eyes so bright? Not with salt tears.
If so, my eyes are oft'ner washed than hers.
No, no, I am as ugly as a bear,   100
For beasts that meet me run away for fear.
Therefore no marvel though Demetrius
Do, as a monster fly my presence thus.
What wicked and dissembling glass of mine
Made me compare with Hermia's sphery eyne?   105
But who is here? Lysander! On the ground!
Dead? or asleep? I see no blood, no wound.
Lysander, if you live, good sir, awake.

LYSANDER [*Waking up*]
And run through fire I will for thy sweet sake.
Transparent Helena! Nature shows art,   110
That through thy bosom makes me see thy heart.
Where is Demetrius? O, how fit a word
Is that vile name to perish on my sword!

HELENA
Do not say so, Lysander; say not so
What though he love your Hermia? Lord, what though?   115
Yet Hermia still loves you. Then be content.

LYSANDER
Content with Hermia! No; I do repent
The tedious minutes I with her have spent.
Not Hermia but Helena I love.
Who will not change a raven for a dove?   120
The will of man is by his reason swayed,
And reason says you are the worthier maid.
Things growing are not ripe until their season
So I, being young, till now ripe not to reason.
And touching now the point of human skill,   125
Reason becomes the marshal to my will
And leads me to your eyes, where I o'erlook
Love's stories written in love's richest book.

129: **wherefore:** why
129: **keen:** sharp
134: **flout my insufficiency:** mock my shortcomings
135: **good troth, good sooth:** (mild oath) indeed
138: **lord of:** possessor or owner
138: **gentleness:** breeding
140: **of:** by
143: **a surfeit:** an excess
145–46: **or as tie heresies . . . they did deceive:** men most despise the false opinions they once believed
149: **address:** apply
157: **removed:** gone (far removed)

Line 157: "Lysander! What, removed? Lysander! Lord!": Olivia de Haviland as Hermia in Dieterle/Reinhardt's 1935 production
Courtesy: Douglas Lanier

159: **an if:** if
160: **of:** for the sake of
161: **nigh:** near

HELENA
    Wherefore was I to this keen mockery born?
    When at your hands did I deserve this scorn?   130
    Is't not enough, is't not enough, young man,
    That I did never, no, nor never can,
    Deserve a sweet look from Demetrius' eye,
    But you must flout my insufficiency?
    Good troth, you do me wrong, good sooth, you do,   135
    In such disdainful manner me to woo.
    But fare you well. Perforce I must confess
    I thought you lord of more true gentleness.
    O, that a lady, of one man refused,
    Should of another therefore be abused!   140

Exit HELENA

LYSANDER
    She sees not Hermia. Hermia, sleep thou there.
    And never mayst thou come Lysander near!
    For as a surfeit of the sweetest things
    The deepest loathing to the stomach brings,
    Or as tie heresies that men do leave   145
    Are hated most of those they did deceive,
    So thou, my surfeit and my heresy,
    Of all be hated, but the most of me!
    And, all my powers, address your love and might
    To honor Helen and to be her knight!   150

Exit LYSANDER

HERMIA [*Waking up*]
    Help me, Lysander, help me! Do thy best
    To pluck this crawling serpent from my breast!
    Ay me, for pity! What a dream was here!
    Lysander, look how I do quake with fear.
    Methought a serpent eat my heart away,   155
    And you sat smiling at his cruel prey.
    Lysander! What, removed? Lysander! Lord!
    What, out of hearing? Gone? No sound, no word?
    Alack, where are you? Speak, an if you hear,
    Speak, of all loves! I swoon almost with fear.   160
    No? Then I well perceive you are not nigh.
    Either death or you I'll find immediately.

Exit

[*A Midsummer Night's Dream*

Act 3

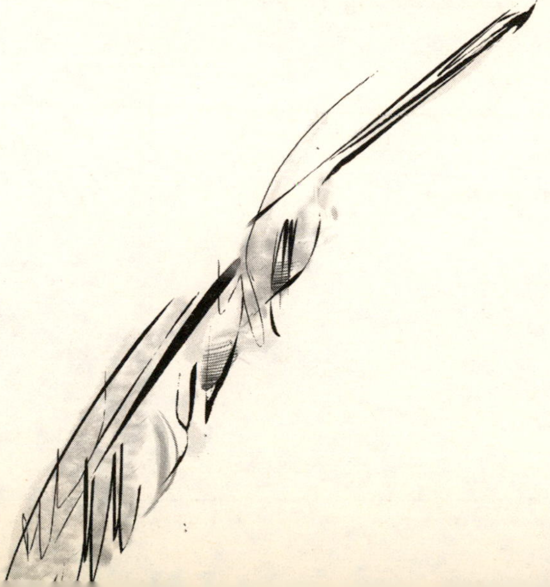

Location: Back in the forest near where Titania sleeps. The craftsmen have come into the forest where they won't be disturbed to rehearse their play, "Pyramus and Thisby."

2: **pat, pat:** right now, on the dot

3: **hawthorn brake:** a thicket of hawthorns

3–4: **tiring house:** dressing room (backstage area)

Scene: Peter Hall's 1968 version, surely the inspiration for Hoffman's rain-soaked forest, was filmed in the late autumn in England on dreary foggy days, creating a depressed and sullen atmosphere for the rehearsal scene. The mechanicals do not "play" with this play; in fact, they are serious in the extreme. Bottom is clearly in competition with Quince and their relationship is antagonistic. Rather than simply overtalking him and attempting to show his expertise in the fine art of playmaking, Hall's Bottom tries to outdo Quince and to embarrass him in front of the other players. When Bottom is transformed, he is utterly and quickly changed into the ass that he emulates. There is no nervous awareness or conceited assumptions. Bottom is quite simply an ass and now he bears the physical manifestations.

6: **bully:** a jolly fellow, though the other meaning is also apt: Bottom bullies weaker personalities

9: **abide:** withstand

10: **By'r lakin':** (an oath) by our lady kin i.e., the Virgin Mary

10: **parlous:** perilous

12: **not a whit:** not in the least

16: **put them out of fear:** i.e., reassure them

TITANIA lying asleep
Enter QUINCE, SNUG, BOTTOM, FLUTE,
SNOUT, and STARVELING

BOTTOM
Are we all met?

QUINCE
Pat, pat; and here's a marvelous convenient place for our rehearsal.
This green plot shall be our stage, this hawthorn brake our tiring
house; and we will do it in action as we will do it before the duke.

BOTTOM
Peter Quince—   5

QUINCE
What sayest thou, bully Bottom?

BOTTOM
There are things in this comedy of Pyramus and Thisby that will
never please. First, Pyramus must draw a sword to kill himself,
which the ladies cannot abide. How answer you that?

SNOUT
By'r lakin, a parlous fear.   10

STARVELING
I believe we must leave the killing out, when all is done.

BOTTOM
Not a whit! I have a device to make all well. Write me a prologue,
and let the prologue seem to say, we will do no harm with our
swords, and that Pyramus is not killed indeed; and, for the more
better assurance, tell them that I, Pyramus, am not Pyramus, but   15
Bottom the weaver. This will put them out of fear.

17-18: eight and six: lines of eight and six syllables, a common ballad meter

Costume for Snug as the Lion from the 1948 staging directed by George Devine
with sets and costumes by Margaret Harris
Rare Book and Special Collections Library, University of Illinois at Urbana-Champaign

23-25: a lion among ladies . . . look to't: at the christening celebrations of Prince
Henry Stuart in Scotland, a blackamoor (i.e., a dark-skinned person) drew the chariot
since the presence of a lion would have frightened some of the people near to it

29: defect: another "Bottomism"; he means to say "effect"

31: my life for yours: I'll risk my life to assure your safety

32: pity of my life: a threat to my life

QUINCE
Well, we will have such a prologue, and it shall be written in eight
and six.

BOTTOM
No, make it two more; let it be written in eight and eight.

SNOUT
Will not the ladies be afeard of the lion?   20

STARVELING
I fear it, I promise you.

BOTTOM
Masters, you ought to consider with yourselves: to bring in—God
shield us!—a lion among ladies is a most dreadful thing, for there
is not a more fearful wildfowl than your lion living, and we ought
to look to't.   25

SNOUT
Therefore another prologue must tell he is not a lion.

BOTTOM
Nay, you must name his name, and half his face must be seen
through the lion's neck, and he himself must speak through,
saying thus, or to the same defect—"Ladies," or "Fair-ladies, I
would wish you," or "I would request you," or "I would entreat   30
you not to fear, not to tremble. My life for yours. If you think I
come hither as a lion, it were pity of my life. No, I am no such
thing; I am a man as other men are." And there indeed let him
name his name and tell them plainly he is Snug, the joiner.

QUINCE
Well it shall be so. But there is two hard things: that is, to bring   35
the moonlight into a chamber, for, you know, Pyramus and
Thisby meet by moonlight.

SNOUT
Doth the moon shine that night we play our play?

44: **a bush of thorns:** a bundle of thornbush kindling—according to popular folklore, part of what the man in the moon carried

45: **disfigure:** Quince misspeaks too—here he means to say "figure," meaning to represent

51: **roughcast:** a plaster made out of gravel and lime

52: **hold his fingers thus:** (the actor usually makes a "V" with his fingers here)

56: **brake:** bush or thicket

58: **hempen homespuns:** peasants or common people easily recognized by their rough, homemade clothing made of hemp

60: **toward:** in production

Scene: In Hoffman's film, Kevin Kline's Bottom attempts to direct the director, Quince, and define himself as the star in the rehearsal for *Pyramus and Thisbe*. He speaks too loudly, he talks over Quince, he insists on being the center of attention. It is not difficult to see why Puck stops mid-flight to work his mischief upon this boorish human.

63–84:
Roy Hudd as Bottom, Richard Cordery as Quince, Richard McCabe as Puck, Alex Lowe as Flute
Warren Mitchell as Bottom, John Moffatt as Quince, Ian Hughes as Puck, Peter Kenny as Flute

tracks 20-22

BOTTOM

A calendar, a calendar! Look in the almanac; find out moonshine,
find out moonshine.   40

QUINCE consults a book

QUINCE

Yes, it doth shine that night.

BOTTOM

Why, then may you leave a casement of the great chamber window,
where we play, open, and the moon may shine in at the casement.

QUINCE

Ay! Or else one must come in with a bush of thorns and a lantern,
and say he comes to disfigure, or to present, the person of   45
Moonshine. Then, there is another thing: we must have a wall in
the great chamber, for Pyramus and Thisby, says the story, did
talk through the chink of a wall.

SNOUT

You can never bring in a wall. What say you, Bottom?

BOTTOM

Some man or other must present Wall, and let him have some   50
plaster, or some loam, or some roughcast about him, to signify
wall, or let him hold his fingers thus, and through that cranny
shall Pyramus and Thisby whisper.

QUINCE

If that may be, then all is well. Come, sit down, every mother's
son, and rehearse your parts. Pyramus, you begin. When you   55
have spoken your speech, enter into that brake and so everyone
according to his cue.

Enter PUCK from behind

PUCK [*Aside*]

What hempen homespuns have we swagg'ring here,
So near the cradle of the fairy queen?
What, a play toward? I'll be an auditor;   60
An actor too, perhaps, if I see cause.

63–84:
Roy Hudd as Bottom, Richard Cordery as Quince, Richard McCabe as Puck, Alex Lowe as Flute
Warren Mitchell as Bottom, John Moffatt as Quince, Ian Hughes as Puck, Peter Kenny as Flute

Unnamed actors as Flute and Bottom. This photograph was taken outside the Shakespeare Memorial Theatre in Stratford-upon-Avon around 1908; the actors are assumed to be from Frank Benson's company
Courtesy: Harry Rusche

75: **brisky juvenal:** a lively and restless youth

75: **eke:** also

75: **Jew:** not in the sense of Jewish, but rather an attempt to rhyme with "hue" (probably short for "juvenal")

77: **Ninny's tomb:** Ninus is the mythical founder of Ninevah. Ninus's wife, Semiramus, built the walls of Babylon, the setting for the story of Pyramus and Thisbe.

79: **part:** script (which then contained only his speeches and cues)

QUINCE
  Speak, Pyramus. Thisby, stand forth.

BOTTOM *as Pyramus*
    Thisby, the flowers of odious savors sweet—

QUINCE
  Odors, odors.

BOTTOM *as Pyramus* [*practicing his lines*]
    Odors savors sweet.   65
    So hath thy breath, my dearest Thisby dear.
    But hark, a voice! Stay thou but here awhile,
    And by and by I will to thee appear.

                                                            Exit

PUCK [*Aside*]
  A stranger Pyramus than e'er played here.

                                                            Exit

FLUTE
  Must I speak now?   70

QUINCE
  Ay, marry, must you; for you must understand he goes but to see
  a noise that he heard and is to come again.

FLUTE *as Thisby*
    Most radiant Pyramus, most lily-white of hue,
    Of color like the red rose on triumphant brier,
    Most brisky juvenal and eke most lovely Jew,   75
    As true as truest horse that yet would never tire!
    I'll meet thee, Pyramus, at Ninny's tomb.

QUINCE
  "Ninus' tomb," man! Why, you must not speak that yet. That, you
  answer to Pyramus. You speak all your part at once, cues and all.
  Pyramus, enter. Your cue is past; it is, "never tire!"   80

tracks 20-22

63–84:
Roy Hudd as Bottom, Richard Cordery as Quince, Richard McCabe as Puck,
Alex Lowe as Flute
Warren Mitchell as Bottom, John Moffatt as Quince, Ian Hughes as Puck,
Peter Kenny as Flute

Stage Direction: **with an ass's head:** This stage direction is from the First Folio, and we infer from this that "the ass's head" was a standard prop

82: **if:** even if

82: **fair:** handsome

82: **were:** would be

Scene: In Reinhardt's film, Puck character experiences a series of transformations. As he sings, he becomes the hound, the boar, and the flame respectively; the "headless bear" was intentionally omitted from the scene by Reinhardt's editors. All the while, Puck remains invisible to the humans who surround him and around whom he dances.

85: **round:** dance in circles

86: **brake:** bush or thicket

88: **a fire:** a will-o'-the-wisp

91: **knavery:** roguish trick

93: **you see an ass-head of your own, do you:** i.e., you must be imagining things

94: **translated:** changed, transformed

FLUTE *as Thisby*
>   *O! As true as truest horse that yet would never tire.*
>   *Reenter PUCK and BOTTOM,*
>   *as Pyramus, with an ass's head*

BOTTOM *as Pyramus*
>   *If I were fair, Thisby, I were only thine.*

QUINCE
>   O monstrous! O strange! We are haunted. Pray, masters! Fly,
>   masters! Help!
>   *Exit QUINCE, SNUG, FLUTE,*
>   *SNOUT, and STARVELING*

PUCK [*dancing around Bottom*]
>   I'll follow you, I'll lead you about a round,   85
>   Through bog, through bush, through brake, through brier.
>   Sometime a horse I'll be, sometime a hound,
>   A hog, a headless bear, sometime a fire;
>   And neigh, and bark, and grunt, and roar, and burn,
>   Like horse, hound, hog, bear, fire, at every turn.   90
>   *Exit*

BOTTOM
>   Why do they run away? This is a knavery of them to make me afeard.
>   *Reenter SNOUT*

SNOUT
>   O Bottom, thou art changed! What do I see on thee?

BOTTOM
>   What do you see? You see an ass-head of your own, do you?
>   *Exit SNOUT*
>   *Reenter QUINCE*

QUINCE
>   Bless thee, Bottom! Bless thee! Thou art translated.
>   *Exit QUINCE*

Scene: James Cagney's Bottom is filled with nervous energy and attention-grabbing buffoonery. He is obnoxious in the extreme and his metamorphosis is equally frenetic in his frightened response. After he slowly and methodically feels his head and his donkey ears and realizes that he has changed, his body begins to tremble uncontrollably. As Bottom sings, he weeps because he realizes that he is now transformed, not into a celebrated actor, but into that most ignominious of animals, an ass. Unlike Cagney, Kline (in Hoffman's 1999 film) does not seem to realize that there has been a change in his appearance, except for his awareness of the need for a shave. The transformation is marvelously subtle. Of particular note is his singing in order to calm his nerves since his fellows have run from him in terror. Every high note turns into a loud "hee-haw" but again, it is a subtle change and could (almost but not quite) be mistaken for a break in his voice.

tracks 23–25

95–132:
Roy Hudd as Bottom, Adjoa Andoh as Titania
Warren Mitchell as Bottom, Sarah Woodward as Titania

99: **ousel cock:** male blackbird

101: **throstle:** song thrush

102: **with little quill:** with a small, high-pitched pipe

105: **the plainsong cuckoo gray:** the gray cuckoo, which sings a simple melody (plainsong)

107: **answer nay:** i.e., deny that he is a cuckold

108: **to so foolish:** to *listen* to so foolish

109: **give a bird the lie:** call a bird a liar

109: **never so:** ever and ever

113: **thy fair virtue's force:** the power of Bottom's beauty or excellence

118: **gleek:** jest

BOTTOM

    I see their knavery. This is to make an ass of me, to fright me, if   95
they could. But I will not stir from this place, do what they can. I
will walk up and down here, and I will sing, that they shall hear
I am not afraid.

                                                  [Sings]

        The ousel cock so black of hue,
        With orange-tawny bill,   100
        The throstle with his note so true,
        The wren with little quill—

TITANIA [*Waking up*]

    What angel wakes me from my flow'ry bed?

BOTTOM

                                                  [Sings]

        The finch, the sparrow and the lark,
        The plainsong cuckoo gray,   105
        Whose note full many a man doth mark,
        And dares not answer nay—
For, indeed, who would set his wit to so foolish a bird? Who
would give a bird the lie, though he cry "cuckoo" never so?

TITANIA

    I pray thee, gentle mortal, sing again.   110
    Mine ear is much enamored of thy note;
    So is mine eye enthrallèd to thy shape;
    And thy fair virtue's force perforce doth move me
    On the first view to say, to swear, I love thee.

BOTTOM

    Methinks, mistress, you should have little reason for that. And 115
yet, to say the truth, reason and love keep little company together
now-a-days; the more the pity that some honest neighbors will not
make them friends. Nay, I can gleek upon occasion.

TITANIA

    Thou art as wise as thou art beautiful.

95–132:
Roy Hudd as Bottom, Adjoa Andoh as Titania
Warren Mitchell as Bottom, Sarah Woodward as Titania

121: **mine own turn:** my purpose

124: **rate:** rank (place in a hierarchy)

Line 126: "And I do love thee!": Catherine Eaton as Titania and Christopher Hutchison as Bottom in the 1999–2000 production at the Guthrie Theater directed by Joe Dowling
Photo: Michal Daniel

125: **still:** always

125: **tend upon my state:** serve me, as one of my royal attendants

130: **purge:** purify or cleanse

130: **grossness:** being or body

Stage Direction: *PEASEBLOSSOM, COBWEB, MOTH, and MUSTARDSEED:* The names of the fairies suggest the tiniest and most delicate, yet durable, things in nature.

BOTTOM

Not so, neither, but if I had wit enough to get out of this wood,   120
I have enough to serve mine own turn.

TITANIA

Out of this wood do not desire to go.
Thou shalt remain here, whether thou wilt or no.
I am a spirit of no common rate;
The summer still doth tend upon my state,   125
And I do love thee! Therefore, go with me;
I'll give thee fairies to attend on thee,
And they shall fetch thee jewels from the deep,
And sing while thou on pressed flowers dost sleep;
And I will purge thy mortal grossness so   130
That thou shalt like an airy spirit go.
Peaseblossom! Cobweb! Moth! And Mustardseed!

Enter PEASEBLOSSOM, COBWEB,
MOTH, and MUSTARDSEED

PEASEBLOSSOM

Ready.

COBWEB

And I.

MOTH

And I.   135

MUSTARDSEED

And I.

ALL

Where shall we go?

Line 137: "Be kind and courteous to this gentleman": James Cagney as Bottom and Anita Louise as Titania in Dieterle/Reinhardt's 1935 production
Courtesy: Douglas Lanier

Scene: Roger Warren writes of Peter Hall's 1968 production that "Judi Dench has the full range of qualities which Titania requires: natural authority, a spontaneous impish sense of humor, and the ability to speak form and verse with both clarity and sensuous beauty...She was particularly successful in communicating that mixture of sensuousness and absurdity both in her infatuated falling in love...and in her instructions to the fairies." Warren goes on to state that Dench could move between love-struck fairy queen and a queen in command of her world.

139: **gambol in his eyes:** dance where he can see you (in order to please him)

140: **dewberries:** blackberries

142: **humblebees:** bumblebees

143: **for night-tapers . . . waxen thighs:** for candles, use bees' legs

145: **to have:** to lead

153: **I cry your worship's mercy:** I beg your pardon

155–56: **If I cut . . . bold with you:** (cobwebs were used like band-aids to stop bleeding)

TITANIA
    Be kind and courteous to this gentleman.
    Hop in his walks and gambol in his eyes;
    Feed him with apricots and dewberries,   140
    With purple grapes, green figs, and mulberries;
    The honeybags steal from the humblebees,
    And for night-tapers crop their waxen thighs
    And light them at the fiery glowworms' eyes,
    To have my love to bed and to arise;   145
    And pluck the wings from painted butterflies
    To fan the moonbeams from his sleeping eyes.
    Nod to him, elves, and do him courtesies.

PEASEBLOSSOM
    Hail, mortal!

COBWEB
    Hail!   150

MOTH
    Hail!

MUSTARDSEED
    Hail!

BOTTOM
    I cry your worship's mercy, heartily. I beseech your worship's name.

COBWEB
    Cobweb.

BOTTOM
    I shall desire you of more acquaintance, good Master Cobweb. If   155
    I cut my finger, I shall make bold with you. Your name, honest
    gentleman?

PEASEBLOSSOM
    Peaseblossom.

159: **Squash:** unripe peapod
160: **Peascod:** ripe peapod, also referring to "codpiece"—a prominent covering for the male genitals
163: **patience:** endurance under suffering
164: **giantlike ox-beef:** dish usually served with mustard or pungent horseradish

Scene: There was no playfulness in Oberon's bewitching of Titania in Brook's 1970 interpretation, thus completely changing the expectations of the play. Titania's mating with Bottom was meant to be graphic and degrading—and it was shown to be.

Line 167: "Come, wait upon him": Ensemble from the 1999–2000 production at the Guthrie Theater directed by Joe Dowling
Photo: Michal Daniel

168: **wat'ry eye:** dew (considered to be a product of the shining moon)
170: **enforcèd:** 1) involuntary   2) violated
171: **Tie up my love's tongue:** make Bottom stop talking (or braying as the case may be)

Scene: In Peter Brook's 1970 production, Bottom is carried to Titania's bower on the shoulders of a male fairy-attendant whose naked arm thrusts upward between Bottom's legs in imitation of a donkey or horse-sized phallus. In Adrian Noble's film, Bottom enters an upside down parasol with Titania and they are both then pulled up beyond the sight of the audience, but the sexual implications are clear. Cagney's ass is sung to sleep by his shimmering white moonbeam of a Titania, and Hoffman's love scene is a fun-filled sexual romp with Pfeiffer's Titania shifting between sitting astride Bottom and then sleepily curling up beside him with her nude leg coiled sexily around Bottom's hairy stomach.

BOTTOM

    I pray you, commend me to Mistress Squash, your mother, and to
Master Peascod, your father. Good Master Peaseblossom, I shall   160
desire you of more acquaintance too. Your name, I beseech you, sir?

MUSTARDSEED

    Mustardseed.

BOTTOM

    Good Master Mustardseed, I know your patience well. That same
cowardly, giantlike ox-beef hath devoured many a gentleman of
your house. I promise you your kindred had made my eyes water ere   165
now. I desire your more acquaintance, good Master Mustardseed.

TITANIA

    Come, wait upon him; lead him to my bower.
The moon methinks looks with a wat'ry eye;
And when she weeps, weeps every little flower,
Lamenting some enforcèd chastity.   170
Tie up my love's tongue. Bring him silently.

Exit All

Location: Still in the forest; towards dawn

3: **in extremity:** to the extreme

5: **mad:** strange, wild

6: **nightrule:** revels or games that take place only at night

6: **haunted:** frequently visited

tracks 26-28

7–35:
Sir John Gielgud as Puck
Ian Hughes as Puck

8: **close:** private

9: **dull:** drowsy

10: **patches:** fools

10: **rude mechanicals:** unpolished (or common) workmen or craftsmen

11: **stalls:** market booths, probably no more than lean-to's

14: **shallowest thick-skin:** silliest oaf

14: **barren:** (referring to non-productive minds) not very smart

15: **Pyramus presented:** acted Pyramus

15: **sport:** play

18: **nole:** (slang) "noodle" meaning head

20: **mimic:** actor

21: **fowler:** hunter (of wild birds)

22: **russet-pated choughs:** gray-headed birds called jackdaws

22: **sort:** a flock

24: **sever:** scatter

26: **stamp:** (Fairies and imps can "stamp" the paths of humans in ways that can interfere with their passage)

28: **lost with their fears:** fearful and thus susceptible to threats, both real and imagined

Act 3, Scene 2]

Enter OBERON

OBERON
    I wonder if Titania be awaked;
    Then, what it was that next came in her eye,
    Which she must dote on in extremity.

Enter PUCK

    Here comes my messenger.
    How now, mad spirit!   5
    What nightrule now about this haunted grove?

PUCK
    My mistress with a monster is in love.
    Near to her close and consecrated bower,
    While she was in her dull and sleeping hour,
    A crew of patches, rude mechanicals,   10
    That work for bread upon Athenian stalls,
    Were met together to rehearse a play
    Intended for great Theseus' nuptial-day.
    The shallowest thick-skin of that barren sort,
    Who Pyramus presented, in their sport   15
    Forsook his scene and entered in a brake.
    When I did him at this advantage take,
    An ass's nole I fixèd on his head.
    Anon his Thisbe must be answerèd,
    And forth my mimic comes. When they him spy,   20
    As wild geese that the creeping fowler eye,
    Or russet-pated choughs, many in sort,
    Rising and cawing at the gun's report,
    Sever themselves and madly sweep the sky,
    So, at his sight, away his fellows fly;   25
    And, at our stamp, here o'er and o'er one falls;
    He "Murder!" cries and help from Athens calls.
    Their sense thus weak, lost with their fears thus strong,

tracks 26-28

7–35:
Sir John Gielgud as Puck
Ian Hughes as Puck

29: senseless: (i.e., without sense) foolish

31: from yielders all things catch: the forest can destroy those who fear the shadows

36–38 Scene: In keeping with Brook's completely non-traditional and modernist production, the "love-in-idleness" nectar is transferred from Puck to Oberon on a spinning plate. Peter Hall, on the other extreme, created an Elizabethan garden within which black-clad figures could move the scenery as needed to emphasize the confusion of the lovers as they chased and then hid from one another in the forest.

37: latched: captured

41: force: necessity

Line 43: "This is the woman, but not this the man": Ensemble from the film of George Balanchine's 1962 ballet
Courtesy: Douglas Lanier

49: o'er shoes: ankle-deep

54: whole: solid

54: bored: pierced

Made senseless, things begin to do them wrong;
For briers and thorns at their apparel snatch;   30
Some sleeves, some hats, from yielders all things catch.
I led them on in this distracted fear,
And left sweet Pyramus translated there.
When in that moment, so it came to pass,
Titania waked and straightway loved an ass.   35

OBERON
This falls out better than I could devise.
But hast thou yet latched the Athenian's eyes
With the love-juice, as I did bid thee do?

PUCK
I took him sleeping—that is finished too—
And the Athenian woman by his side,   40
That, when he waked, of force she must be eyed.

Enter HERMIA and DEMETRIUS

OBERON
Stand close. This is the same Athenian.

PUCK
This is the woman, but not this the man.

DEMETRIUS
O, why rebuke you him that loves you so?
Lay breath so bitter on your bitter foe.   45

HERMIA
Now I but chide, but I should use thee worse,
For thou, I fear, hast given me cause to curse
If thou hast slain Lysander in his sleep,
Being o'er shoes in blood, plunge in the deep
And kill me too.   50
The sun was not so true unto the day
As he to me. Would he have stolen away
From sleeping Hermia? I'll believe as soon
This whole earth may be bored and that the moon

55: displease: disrupt

56: her brother's noontide with th'Antipodes: noontime on the other side of the Earth (where the Antipodes are located, relative to London)

58: so dead: pale as death

62: Venus: Roman goddess of love and beauty; also, the planet Venus

62: glimmering sphere: orbit

63: to: about

69: once tell true: once and for all

70: being awake: when he was awake

71: brave touch: noble stroke (in sarcastic tone)

72: worm: serpent

73: adder: serpent (one of the deadliest)

75: misprised mood: misplaced anger

79: and if: if

79: therefore: for that

May through the centre creep and so displease   55
Her brother's noontide with th'Antipodes.
It cannot be but thou hast murdered him.
So should a murderer look, so dead, so grim.

DEMETRIUS
So should the murdered look, and so should I,
Pierced through the heart with your stern cruelty.   60
Yet you, the murderer, look as bright, as clear,
As yonder Venus in her glimmering sphere.

HERMIA
What's this to my Lysander? Where is he?
Ah, good Demetrius, wilt thou give him me?

DEMETRIUS
I had rather give his carcass to my hounds.   65

HERMIA
Out, dog! Out, cur! Thou driv'st me past the bounds
Of maiden's patience. Hast thou slain him, then?
Henceforth be never numbered among men!
O, once tell true, tell true, even for my sake!
Durst thou have looked upon him being awake,   70
And hast thou killed him sleeping? O brave touch!
Could not a worm, an adder, do so much?
An adder did it; for with doubler tongue
Than thine, thou serpent, never adder stung.

DEMETRIUS
You spend your passion on a misprised mood.   75
I am not guilty of Lysander's blood;
Nor is he dead, for aught that I can tell.

HERMIA
I pray thee, tell me then that he is well.

DEMETRIUS
And if I could, what should I get therefore?

83: **vein:** state of mind

85: **heaviness:** sadness

86: **for debt . . . sorrow owe:** i.e., sleeplessness owes much to sorrow

88: **if for his tender here I make some stay:** i.e., I'm going to try to reclaim some of that lost sleep.

91: **misprision:** mistake

92: **turned:** changed, switched

Lines 93–94: "Then fate o'errules, that, one man holding troth, / A million fail, confounding oath on oath": Morgan Freeman as Puck in the 1974 production by The Public Theater directed by Edward Berkeley

Photo: George E. Joseph

93–94: **Then fate . . . oath on oath:** Fate governs all, because for every man who keeps a promise, a million will fail

93: **holding troth:** being true (faithful)

96: **look thou:** you must

97: **fancy-sick:** lovesick

98: **sighs of love . . . blood dear:** (every sigh was thought to cost a drop of blood)

100: **against she do appear:** in preparation for her arrival

102: **Tartar's bow:** (Tartars from Asia Minor were expert archers)

HERMIA

A privilege never to see me more.   80
And from thy hated presence part I so.
See me no more, whether he be dead or no.

Exit

DEMETRIUS

There is no following her in this fierce vein.
Here, therefore, for a while I will remain.
So sorrow's heaviness doth heavier grow   85
For debt that bankrupt sleep doth sorrow owe,
Which now in some slight measure it will pay,
If for his tender here I make some stay.

Lies down and sleeps
OBERON and PUCK come forward

OBERON

What hast thou done? Thou hast mistaken quite
And laid the love-juice on some true-love's sight.   90
Of thy misprision must perforce ensue
Some true love turned and not a false turned true.

PUCK

Then fate o'errules, that, one man holding troth,
A million fail, confounding oath on oath.

OBERON

About the wood go swifter than the wind,   95
And Helena of Athens look thou find.
All fancy-sick she is and pale of cheer,
With sighs of love, that costs the fresh blood dear.
By some illusion see thou bring her here.
I'll charm his eyes against she do appear.   100

PUCK

I go, I go; look how I go,
Swifter than arrow from the Tartar's bow.

Exit

Stage Direction: [*applying the nectar to Demetrius' eyes*]: Paul Whitthorne as
Demetrius and Mark H. Dold as Oberon in the Shakespeare Theatre Company's
2003–04 production directed by Mark Lamos
Photo: Richard Termine

105: **apple:** pupil

106: **his love:** refers to Helena

108: **Venus:** the planet Venus, one of the brightest objects in the sky

114: **fee:** reward

115: **fond pageant:** silly spectacle

120: **sport alone:** a unique game

122: **befall prepost'rously:** 1) come about unnaturally   2) are unnatural or unusual
events

125–26: **vows so born . . . all truth appears:** vows pledged through tears are sincere

128: **the badge of faith:** i.e., my tearful profession

OBERON [*applying the nectar to Demetrius' eyes*]
  Flower of this purple dye,
  Hit with Cupid's archery,
  Sink in apple of his eye.   105
  When his love he doth espy,
  Let her shine as gloriously
  As the Venus of the sky.
  When thou wak'st, if she be by,
  Beg of her for remedy.   110
             Reenter PUCK

PUCK
 Captain of our fairy band,
 Helena is here at hand;
 And the youth, mistook by me,
 Pleading for a lover's fee.
 Shall we their fond pageant see?   115
 Lord, what fools these mortals be!

OBERON
 Stand aside! The noise they make
 Will cause Demetrius to awake.

PUCK
 Then will two at once woo one;
 That must needs be sport alone;   120
 And those things do best please me
 That befall prepost'rously.

       Enter LYSANDER and HELENA

LYSANDER
 Why should you think that I should woo in scorn?
 Scorn and derision never come in tears.
 Look, when I vow, I weep; and vows so born, 125
 In their nativity all truth appears.
 How can these things in me seem scorn to you,
 Bearing the badge of faith, to prove them true?

129: **advance:** display

130: **truth kills truth:** one vow cancels the other

130: **devilish-holy:** ("devilish" because truth is being conquered; "holy" because truth is the conqueror)

131: **give her o'er:** give her over i.e., give her up

134: **tales:** lies

Line 137: "Demetrius loves her, and he loves not you": Paris Remillard as Lysander and Kate Nowlin as Helena in the Shakespeare Theatre Company's 2003–04 production directed by Mark Lamos

Photo: Richard Termine

139: **eyne:** eyes

140: **show:** appearance

142: **Taurus snow:** mountain range in Asia Minor where Tartars dwell

143: **turns to a crow:** looks black in contrast to the snow

145: **seal:** promise, pledge

147: **to set against:** to attack

151: **join in souls:** become one force

154: **superpraise:** (too much praise seems insincere)

154: **parts:** qualities

HELENA
    You do advance your cunning more and more.
    When truth kills truth, O devilish-holy fray!   130
    These vows are Hermia's. Will you give her o'er?
    Weigh oath with oath, and you will nothing weigh.
    Your vows to her and me, put in two scales,
    Will even weigh, and both as light as tales.

LYSANDER
    I had no judgment when to her I swore.   135

HELENA
    Nor none, in my mind, now you give her o'er.

LYSANDER
    Demetrius loves her, and he loves not you.

DEMETRIUS [*Waking up*]
    O Helena, goddess, nymph, perfect, divine!
    To what, my love, shall I compare thine eyne?
    Crystal is muddy. O, how ripe in show   140
    Thy lips, those kissing cherries, tempting grow!
    That pure congealèd white, high Taurus snow,
    Fanned with the eastern wind, turns to a crow
    When thou hold'st up thy hand. O, let me kiss
    This princess of pure white, this seal of bliss!   145

HELENA
    O spite! O hell! I see you all are bent
    To set against me for your merriment.
    If you were civil and knew courtesy,
    You would not do me thus much injury.
    Can you not hate me, as I know you do,   150
    But you must join in souls to mock me too?
    If you were men, as men you are in show,
    You would not use a gentle lady so;
    To vow, and swear, and superpraise my parts,
    When I am sure you hate me with your hearts.   155
    You both are rivals, and love Hermia;

158: trim: fine, pretty (the complete line is frequently delivered with a sneer)

160: sort: rank

161: extort: force, twist

162: make you sport: entertain yourselves

166: my part: i.e., my feelings of love

Line 169: "Never did mockers waste more idle breath": Rick Lieberman as Demetrius, Christine Baranski as Helena, and Kevin Conroy as Lysander in The Public Theater's 1981–82 production directed by James Lapine
Photo: George E. Joseph

170: I will none: I don't want any part of this game

172: but as guestwise sojourned: i.e., was like a guest's visit: temporary

176: aby it dear: pay dearly for it

And now both rivals, to mock Helena.
A trim exploit, a manly enterprise,
To conjure tears up in a poor maid's eyes
With your derision! None of noble sort   160
Would so offend a virgin and extort
A poor soul's patience, all to make you sport.

LYSANDER
You are unkind, Demetrius; be not so,
For you love Hermia; this you know I know.
And here, with all good will, with all my heart,   165
In Hermia's love I yield you up my part;
And yours of Helena to me bequeath,
Whom I do love and will do till my death.

HELENA
Never did mockers waste more idle breath.

DEMETRIUS
Lysander, keep thy Hermia; I will none.   170
If e'er I loved her, all that love is gone.
My heart to her but as guestwise sojourned,
And now to Helen is it home returned,
There to remain.

LYSANDER
                    Helen, it is not so.

DEMETRIUS
Disparage not the faith thou dost not know,   175
Lest, to thy peril, thou aby it dear.
Look, where thy love comes; yonder is thy dear.

                                        Reenter HERMIA

188: **engilds the night:** shines in the night, like silver and gold

189: **fiery oes:** bright stars

194: **conjoined all three:** all three united

195: **false sport:** wicked game

195: **in spite of me:** just to make me mad

198: **to bait me:** to tease me

199: **counsel:** sharing secrets

201: **chid:** chided

204: **artificial:** artistically gifted

HERMIA

    Dark night, that from the eye his function takes,
    The ear more quick of apprehension makes;
    Wherein it doth impair the seeing sense,   180
    It pays the hearing double recompense.
    Thou art not by mine eye, Lysander, found;
    Mine ear, I thank it, brought me to thy sound.
    But why unkindly didst thou leave me so?

LYSANDER

    Why should he stay, whom love doth press to go?   185

HERMIA

    What love could press Lysander from my side?

LYSANDER

    Lysander's love, that would not let him bide,
    Fair Helena, who more engilds the night
    Than all you fiery oes and eyes of light.
    Why seek'st thou me? Could not this make thee know,   190
    The hate I bear thee made me leave thee so?

HERMIA

    You speak not as you think. It cannot be.

HELENA

    Lo, she is one of this confederacy!
    Now I perceive they have conjoined all three
    To fashion this false sport, in spite of me.   195
    Injurious Hermia! Most ungrateful maid!
    Have you conspired, have you with these contrived
    To bait me with this foul derision?
    Is all the counsel that we two have shared,
    The sisters' vows, the hours that we have spent,   200
    When we have chid the hasty-footed time
    For parting us—O, is it all forgot?
    All schooldays' friendship, childhood innocence?
    We, Hermia, like two artificial gods,
    Have with our needles created both one flower,   205

207: in one key: i.e., in perfect harmony

209: incorporate: as one body

214–15: two of the first . . . with one crest: two bodies but one identity

216: rent: rip

216: ancient: long-standing

Lines 223–224: "Have you not set Lysander, as in scorn, / To follow me and praise my eyes and face?": Noel True as Hermia, Paul Whitthorne as Demetrius, Kate Nowlin as Helena, and Paris Remillard as Lysander in the Shakespeare Theatre Company's 2003–04 production directed by Mark Lamos
Photo: Richard Termine

226: even but: just

226: spurn: kick

231: tender: offer

232: setting on: encouragement

233: grace: favor

Both on one sampler, sitting on one cushion,
Both warbling of one song, both in one key,
As if our hands, our sides, voices and minds,
Had been incorporate. So we grow together,
Like to a double cherry, seeming parted,   210
But yet an union in partition,
Two lovely berries moulded on one stem;
So, with two seeming bodies, but one heart,
Two of the first, like coats in heraldry,
Due but to one and crownèd with one crest.   215
And will you rent our ancient love asunder,
To join with men in scorning your poor friend?
It is not friendly, 'tis not maidenly.
Our sex, as well as I, may chide you for it,
Though I alone do feel the injury.   220

HERMIA
    I am amazed at your passionate words.
    I scorn you not. It seems that you scorn me.

HELENA
    Have you not set Lysander, as in scorn,
    To follow me and praise my eyes and face?
    And made your other love, Demetrius,   225
    Who even but now did spurn me with his foot,
    To call me goddess, nymph, divine and rare,
    Precious, celestial? Wherefore speaks he this
    To her he hates? And wherefore doth Lysander
    Deny your love, so rich within his soul,   230
    And tender me, forsooth, affection,
    But by your setting on, by your consent?
    What thought I be not so in grace as you,
    So hung upon with love, so fortunate,
    But miserable most, to love unloved?   235
    This you should pity rather than despise.

HERMIA
    I understand not what you mean by this.

238: **persever:** try harder (i.e., persevere)

238: **counterfeit sad looks:** pretending to be serious

239: **make mouths upon:** make faces at

240: **hold the sweet jest:** carry on or keep up the joke

241: **well carried:** well done

243: **argument:** object of the tricks

249: **her:** referring to Helena

250: **she:** referring to Hermia

250: **entreat:** persuade you to stop

250: **compel:** make you stop

254: **that which I will lose for thee:** i.e., my life

257: **prove it too:** prove your claim in a duel

HELENA
    Ay, do. Persever, counterfeit sad looks,
    Make mouths upon me when I turn my back,
    Wink each at other, hold the sweet jest up.   240
    This sport, well carried, shall be chronicled.
    If you have any pity, grace, or manners,
    You would not make me such an argument.
    But fare ye well: 'tis partly my own fault;
    Which death or absence soon shall remedy.   245

LYSANDER
    Stay, gentle Helena; hear my excuse,
    My love, my life, my soul, fair Helena!

HELENA
    O excellent!

HERMIA [*to Lysander*]
    Sweet, do not scorn her so.

DEMETRIUS [*to Lysander*]
    If she cannot entreat, I can compel.   250

LYSANDER
    Thou canst compel no more than she entreat.
    Thy threats have no more strength than her weak prayers.
    Helen, I love thee; by my life, I do.
    I swear by that which I will lose for thee,
    To prove him false that says I love thee not.   255

DEMETRIUS
    I say I love thee more than he can do.

LYSANDER
    If thou say so, withdraw, and prove it too.

DEMETRIUS
    Quick, come!

259: Ethiope: an Ethiopian—referring to Hermia's dark hair and eyes

260: take on as: make as if

Line 262: "Hang off, thou cat, thou burr!": Rick Lieberman as Demetrius, Christine Baranski as Helena, Kevin Conroy as Lysander, and Deborah Rush as Hermia in The Public Theater's 1981–82 production directed by James Lapine
Photo: George E. Joseph

262: hang off: let go

265: tawny Tartar: refers to Hermia (Tartars have dark complexions)

266: loathèd med'cine: poison

267: sooth: truly

270: weak bond: refers to Demetrius's untrustworthiness and also to Hermia's hold on Lysander

HERMIA
                    Lysander, whereto tends all this?

LYSANDER
    Away, you Ethiope!

DEMETRIUS
                    No, no; he'll...
    Seem to break loose; take on as you would follow,   260
    But yet come not. You are a tame man, go!

LYSANDER [*to Hermia*]
    Hang off, thou cat, thou burr! Vile thing, let loose,
    Or I will shake thee from me like a serpent!

HERMIA
    Why are you grown so rude? What change is this?
    Sweet love—

LYSANDER
                    Thy love! Out, tawny Tartar, out!   265
    Out, loathèd med'cine! O, hated potion, hence!

HERMIA
    Do you not jest?

HELENA
                    Yes, sooth, and so do you.

LYSANDER
    Demetrius, I will keep my word with thee.

DEMETRIUS
    I would I had your bond, for I perceive
    A weak bond holds you. I'll not trust your word.   270

LYSANDER
    What, should I hurt her, strike her, kill her dead?
    Although I hate her, I'll not harm her so.

274: **wherefore:** why

274: **what news:** what is the matter?

276: **erewhile:** a little while ago

279: **in earnest, shall I say:** i.e., I speak in earnest

284: **juggler:** trickster

284: **cankerblossom:** a worm that destroys blossoms (representing destroyed love)

290: **puppet:** hollow imitation

291: **puppet:** (Hermia takes this as a pejorative regarding her small stature)

298: **painted maypole:** (Hermia hurls this insult at the taller Helena)

Kate Nowlin as Helena, Noel True as Hermia, Daniel Breaker as Puck, and Mark H. Dold as Oberon in the Shakespeare Theatre Company's 2003-04 production directed by Mark Lamos

Photo: Richard Termine

HERMIA

What, can you do me greater harm than hate?
Hate me! Wherefore? O me! What news, my love!
Am not I Hermia? Are not you Lysander?   275
I am as fair now as I was erewhile.
Since night you loved me; yet since night you left me.
Why, then you left me—O, the gods forbid!—
In earnest, shall I say?

LYSANDER

     Ay, by my life;
And never did desire to see thee more.   280
Therefore be out of hope, of question, of doubt;
Be certain, nothing truer; 'tis no jest
That I do hate thee and love Helena.

HERMIA

O me! You juggler! You cankerblossom!
You thief of love! What, have you come by night   285
And stolen my love's heart from him?

HELENA

    Fine, i' faith!
Have you no modesty, no maiden shame,
No touch of bashfulness? What, will you tear
Impatient answers from my gentle tongue?
Fie, fie! You counterfeit, you puppet, you!   290

HERMIA

Puppet? Why so? Ay, that way goes the game.
Now I perceive that she hath made compare
Between our statures; she hath urged her height,
And with her personage, her tall personage,
Her height, forsooth, she hath prevailed with him.   295
And are you grown so high in his esteem,
Because I am so dwarfish and so low?
How low am I, thou painted maypole? Speak!
How low am I? I am not yet so low
But that my nails can reach unto thine eyes.   300

301–346:
Saskia Wickham as Helena, Amanda Root as Hermia, Rupert Penry-Jones
as Lysander, Clarence Smith as Demetrius
Emily Raymond as Helena, Cathy Sara as Hermia, Benjamin Soames
as Lysander, Jamie Glover as Demetrius

302: **curst:** quarrelsome

304: **right:** proper

306: **something:** somewhat

312: **your stealth:** your sneaking or running away

314: **hath chid me hence:** has driven me away with his insults (chiding)

315: **spurn:** kick

316: **so:** if

319: **fond:** foolish

323: **she:** refers to Hermia

HELENA

    I pray you, though you mock me, gentlemen,
    Let her not hurt me. I was never curst;
    I have no gift at all in shrewishness;
    I am a right maid for my cowardice.
    Let her not strike me. You perhaps may think,   305
    Because she is something lower than myself,
    That I can match her.

HERMIA

              "Lower"? Hark, again.

HELENA

    Good Hermia, do not be so bitter with me.
    I evermore did love you, Hermia,
    Did ever keep your counsels, never wronged you,   310
    Save that, in love unto Demetrius,
    I told him of your stealth unto this wood.
    He followed you; for love I followed him;
    But he hath chid me hence and threatened me
    To strike me, spurn me, nay, to kill me too.   315
    And now, so you will let me quiet go,
    To Athens will I bear my folly back
    And follow you no further. Let me go!
    You see how simple and how fond I am.

HERMIA

    Why, get you gone. Who is't that hinders you?   320

HELENA

    A foolish heart, that I leave here behind.

HERMIA

    What, with Lysander?

HELENA

              With Demetrius.

LYSANDER

    Be not afraid; she shall not harm thee, Helena.

tracks 29-31

301–346:
Saskia Wickham as Helena, Amanda Root as Hermia, Rupert Penry-Jones
as Lysander, Clarence Smith as Demetrius
Emily Raymond as Helena, Cathy Sara as Hermia, Benjamin Soames
as Lysander, Jamie Glover as Demetrius

324: **she:** refers to Hermia

324: **her:** refers to Helena

325: **keen:** a sharp tongue

325: **shrewd:** a shrew

329: **suffer:** permit

329: **flout:** insult

331: **minimus:** small creature

331: **hind'ring knot-grass:** weed (thought to stunt growth)

332: **bead:** tiny thing

332: **officious:** attentive, obliging

335: **intend:** mean

337: **aby:** pay for

340: **cheek by jowl:** side by side

341: **coil:** turmoil

341: **long:** because of

342: **go not back:** do not retreat

DEMETRIUS

No, sir, she shall not, though you take her part.

HELENA

O, when she's angry, she is keen and shrewd!   325
She was a vixen when she went to school,
And though she be but little, she is fierce.

HERMIA

"Little" again? Nothing but "low" and "little"?
Why will you suffer her to flout me thus?
Let me come to her.

LYSANDER

                    Get you gone, you dwarf!   330
You minimus of hind'ring knot-grass made!
You bead! You acorn—

DEMETRIUS

                    You are too officious
In her behalf that scorns your services.
Let her alone. Speak not of Helena.
Take not her part, for if thou dost intend   335
Never so little show of love to her,
Thou shalt aby it.

LYSANDER

                    Now she holds me not;
Now follow, if thou darest, to try whose right,
Of thine or mine, is most in Helena.

DEMETRIUS

Follow! Nay, I'll go with thee, cheek by jowl.   340
                    Exit LYSANDER and DEMETRIUS

HERMIA

You, mistress, all this coil is long of you.
Nay, go not back.

tracks 29-31

301–346:
*Saskia Wickham as Helena, Amanda Root as Hermia, Rupert Penry-Jones
as Lysander, Clarence Smith as Demetrius
Emily Raymond as Helena, Cathy Sara as Hermia, Benjamin Soames
as Lysander, Jamie Glover as Demetrius*

343: **curst:** quarrelsome
344: **fray:** fight
347: **still thou:** you always
348: **knaveries:** roguish tricks
349: **shadows:** fairies and spirits of the night
352: **and so:** therefore
354: **so did sort:** turned out this way
355: **jangling:** bickering

tracks 32-34

356–379:
*Sir John Gielgud as Oberon
Michael Maloney as Oberon*

357: **hie:** Hurry up
358: **welkin:** sky
359: **Acheron:** a river in Hades
361: **as:** So that
362: **Like to Lysander sometime frame thy tongue:** fashion your speech after
Lysander, i.e., talk and sound like Lysander
363: **wrong:** insults
365: **look thou:** make sure you
367: **batty:** batlike
368: **this herb:** the antidote to Cupid's flower, love-in-idleness (see line 2.1.168)
369: **virtuous:** potent
370: **his might:** its strength

HELENA
                    I will not trust you, I,
    Nor longer stay in your curst company.
    Your hands than mine are quicker for a fray,
    My legs are longer though, to run away.   345

                                                                    Exit

HERMIA
    I am amazed, and know not what to say.

                                                                    Exit

OBERON
    This is thy negligence. Still thou mistak'st
    Or else committ'st thy knaveries wilfully.

PUCK
    Believe me, king of shadows, I mistook.
    Did not you tell me I should know the man   350
    By the Athenian garment be had on?
    And so far blameless proves my enterprise,
    That I have 'nointed an Athenian's eyes;
    And so far am I glad it so did sort,
    As this their jangling I esteem a sport.   355

OBERON
    Thou see'st these lovers seek a place to fight.
    Hie therefore, Robin, overcast the night;
    The starry welkin cover thou anon
    With drooping fog as black as Acheron,
    And lead these testy rivals so astray   360
    As one come not within another's way.
    Like to Lysander sometime frame thy tongue,
    Then stir Demetrius up with bitter wrong.
    And sometime rail thou like Demetrius,
    And from each other look thou lead them thus,   365
    Till o'er their brows death-counterfeiting sleep
    With leaden legs and batty wings doth creep.
    Then crush this herb into Lysander's eye;

                                              Gives flower to PUCK

    Whose liquor hath this virtuous property,
    To take from thence all error with his might,   370

356–379:
Sir John Gielgud as Oberon
Michael Maloney as Oberon

371: **wonted:** normal
372: **derision:** mockery
373: **fruitless:** inconsequential
374: **wend:** go
375: **league:** covenant, promise
375: **date:** term of contract
378: **charmèd eye:** enchanted gaze
381: **night's swift dragons:** the winged dragons that pull the chariot of night
382: **Aurora's harbinger:** the planet Venus, also known as the morning star, heralds the dawn, Aurora
384–385: **damnèd spirits . . . have burial:** (those who die traveling or at sea remain unburied by their families and are condemned to wander between the land of the living and the land of the dead, belonging to neither world)
388: **exile from light:** (the spirit world must avoid contact with daylight)
389: **for aye:** forever
391: **morning's love:** Aurora's lover, Cephalus
392: **forester:** keeper of the royal forest
395: **his salt green streams:** the sea

Scene: Puck flits about between the young men, luring them by imitating Lysander to Demetrius and Demetrius to Lysander, leading Helena and Hermia to the same spot, and then casting his spell, causing them to fall asleep: Lysander near Hermia and Demetrius near Helena.

401: **Goblin:** hobgoblin (Puck is addressing himself)

And make his eyeballs roll with wonted sight.
When they next wake, all this derision
Shall seem a dream and fruitless vision,
And back to Athens shall the lovers wend,
With league whose date till death shall never end.   375
Whiles I in this affair do thee employ,
I'll to my queen and beg her Indian boy;
And then I will her charmèd eye release
From monster's view, and all things shall be peace.

PUCK

My fairy lord, this must be done with haste,   380
For night's swift dragons cut the clouds full fast,
And yonder shines Aurora's harbinger,
At whose approach, ghosts, wand'ring here and there,
Troop home to churchyards. Damnèd spirits all,
That in crossways and floods have burial,   385
Already to their wormy beds are gone.
For fear lest day should look their shames upon,
They willfully themselves exile from light
And must for aye consort with black-browed night.

OBERON

But we are spirits of another sort.   390
I with the morning's love have oft made sport,
And, like a forester, the groves may tread
Even till the eastern gate, all fiery-red,
Opening on Neptune with fair blessed beams,
Turns into yellow gold his salt green streams.   395
But, notwithstanding, haste; make no delay.
We may effect this business yet ere day.

                                                        Exit

PUCK

        Up and down, up and down,
        I will lead them up and down.
        I am feared in field and town.   400
        Goblin, lead them up and down.
Here comes one.

                                        Reenter LYSANDER

404: **drawn:** my sword is drawn

406: **plainer:** less dense (with foliage)

411: **recreant:** cowardly wretch

414: **try:** test

415: **still:** continuously

Oberon's lair in the woods. Set rendering from the March 23, 1954 staging at the Shakespeare Memorial Theatre (Stratford-upon-Avon, England) directed by George Devine with sets and costumes by Margaret Harris

LYSANDER
  Where art thou, proud Demetrius? Speak thou now.

PUCK [*in Demetrius' voice*]
  Here, villain; drawn and ready. Where art thou?

LYSANDER
  I will be with thee straight.

PUCK [*in Demetrius' voice*]
                    Follow me, then,   405
  To plainer ground.
                    Exit LYSANDER, following the voice
                    Reenter DEMETRIUS

DEMETRIUS
                    Lysander! Speak again.
  Thou runaway, thou coward, art thou fled?
  Speak! In some bush? Where dost thou hide thy head?

PUCK [*in Lysander's voice*]
  Thou coward, art thou bragging to the stars?
  Telling the bushes that thou look'st for wars   410
  And wilt not come? Come, recreant! Come, thou child!
  I'll whip thee with a rod. He is defiled
  That draws a sword on thee.

DEMETRIUS
                    Yea, art thou there?

PUCK [*in Lysander's voice*]
  Follow my voice. We'll try no manhood here.
                    Exit PUCK and DEMETRIUS
                    Reenter LYSANDER

LYSANDER
  He goes before me and still dares me on.   415
  When I come where he calls, then he is gone.
  The villain is much lighter-heeled than I.

419: **that:** thus

424: **abide:** Wait for

424: **wot:** know

428: **buy this:** pay for this

428: **dear:** dearly

431: **measure out my length:** i.e., stretch out or lie down

431: **this cold bed:** i.e., the ground

434: **abate:** Shorten

Mickey Rooney as Puck with the fairy attendants in Dieterle/Reinhardt's 1935 production
Courtesy: Douglas Lanier

I followed fast, but faster he did fly;
That fallen am I in dark uneven way,
And here will rest me.

Lies down

                    Come, thou gentle day!   420
For if but once thou show me thy grey light,
I'll find Demetrius and revenge this spite.

Sleeps
Reenter PUCK and DEMETRIUS

PUCK [*in Lysander's voice*]
Ho, ho, ho! Coward, why com'st thou not?

DEMETRIUS
Abide me, if thou dar'st, for well I wot
Thou runn'st before me, shifting every place,   425
And dar'st not stand, nor look me in the face.
Where art thou now?

PUCK [*in Lysander's voice*]
                    Come hither. I am here.

DEMETRIUS
Nay, then, thou mock'st me. Thou shalt buy this dear,
If ever I thy face by daylight see.
Now, go thy way. Faintness constraineth me   430
To measure out my length on this cold bed.
By day's approach look to be visited.

Lies down and sleeps
Reenter HELENA

HELENA
O weary night, O long and tedious night,
Abate thy hours? Shine comforts from the east,
That I may back to Athens by daylight,   435
From these that my poor company detest.
And sleep, that sometimes shuts up sorrow's eye,
Steal me awhile from mine own company.

Lies down and sleeps

441: **curst:** angry

445: **bedabbled:** dampened

463: **Jack shall have Jill:** the boy and the girl will be matched properly

465: **the man shall have his mare:** as in line 463

465: **all shall be well:** the proper order of the cosmos is restored

Scene: In Hoffman's film, Rupert Everett's Oberon works to correct Puck's mistake. He hovers near the lovers dropping "flower of this purple dye." He is almost too beautiful, almost too Dionysian. Yet, his understated and unintimidating Oberon makes sense here as he administers a kindness not very likely in the pucks and goblins of English folklore.

PUCK

>Yet but three? Come one more;
>Two of both kinds make up four.   440
>Here she comes, curst and sad.
>Cupid is a knavish lad,
>Thus to make poor females mad.

Reenter HERMIA

HERMIA

Never so weary, never so in woe,
Bedabbled with the dew and torn with briers,   445
I can no further crawl, no further go;
My legs can keep no pace with my desires.
Here will I rest me till the break of day.
Heavens shield Lysander, if they mean a fray!

Lies down and sleeps

PUCK

>On the ground   450
>Sleep sound.
>I'll apply
>To your eye,
>Gentle lover, remedy.

Squeezing the nectar on LYSANDER's eyelids

>When thou wak'st,   455
>Thou tak'st
>True delight
>In the sight
>Of thy former lady's eye.
>And the country proverb known,   460
>That every man should take his own,
>In your waking shall be shown.
>Jack shall have Jill;
>Nought shall go ill;
The man shall have his mare again, and all shall be well. 465

Exit

[*A Midsummer Night's Dream*

Act 4

Location: Still in the forest. The lovers lie together, sound asleep. The fairies enter to attend Titania who prepares for bed with Bottom. Oberon watches but remains invisible to the fairies.

2: **amiable:** lovely

2: **coy:** caress

13: **overflown:** covered

Ernest Cossart as Bottom. Possibly from a 1915 production at Wallack's Theatre in New York City directed by Granville Barker
Courtesy: Harry Rusche

LYSANDER, DEMETRIUS, HELENA,
and HERMIA lying asleep
Enter TITANIA and BOTTOM, PEASEBLOSSOM, COBWEB,
MOTH, MUSTARDSEED, and other fairies
OBERON behind, unseen

TITANIA
    Come, sit thee down upon this flowery bed,
    While I thy amiable cheeks do coy,
    And stick muskroses in thy sleek smooth head,
    And kiss thy fair large ears, my gentle joy.

BOTTOM
    Where's Peaseblossom? 5

PEASEBLOSSOM
    Ready.

BOTTOM
    Scratch my head Peaseblossom. Where's Monsieur Cobweb?

COBWEB
    Ready.

BOTTOM
    Monsieur Cobweb, good monsieur, get you your weapons in your
    hand and kill me a red-hipped humble-bee on the top of a thistle; 10
    and, good monsieur, bring me the honey-bag. Do not fret yourself
    too much in the action, monsieur; and, good monsieur, have a care
    the honey-bag break not; I would be loath to have you overflown
    with a honey-bag, signor. Where's Monsieur Mustardseed?

MUSTARDSEED
    Ready. 15

16: **neaf:** fist

16–17: **leave your courtesy:** stop bowing

19: **Cavalry Cobweb:** Bottom mistakes Peaseblossom for Cobweb and calls "Cobweb" a gentleman, mistaking "Cavalry" for "Cavalier," a formal address for a gentleman

20: **marvelous:** marvelously

24–25: **tongs and bones:** rustic musical instruments made of bones and (probably) spoons; stage direction in the First Folio reads: *Music: tongs, rural music*

Scene: At this point in the play, Bottom has been transformed in more than one way, as most productions do not hesitate to show. In Hoffman's film, Bottom's call for a "peck of provender" is accompanied by smacking, yawning, and scratching. Michelle Pfeiffer as Titania is not deterred by this behavior and, in fact, dotes on it, ordering the fairy attendants to bring Bottom whatever he desires. In Reinhardt's production, Titania sings Bottom to sleep, petting his long ears, while Oberon waits nearby and the fairies dance around like fairy dust.

27: **peck of provender:** a quarter bushel of grain (another of Bottom's rural colloquialisms)

28: **bottle:** Bottom means a "bundle"

29: **fellow:** equal

30: **venturous:** one who ventures forth

33: **stir:** disturb

33: **exposition of:** Bottomism for "disposition to"

BOTTOM
Give me your neaf, Monsieur Mustardseed. Pray you, leave your
courtesy, good monsieur.

MUSTARDSEED
What's your will?

BOTTOM
Nothing, good monsieur, but to help Cavalry Cobweb to scratch.
I must to the barber's, monsieur, for methinks I am marvelous   20
hairy about the face. And I am such a tender ass, if my hair do but
tickle me, I must scratch.

TITANIA
What, wilt thou hear some music, my sweet love?

BOTTOM
I have a reasonable good ear in music. Let's have the tongs and
the bones.   25

TITANIA
Or say, sweet love, what thou desirest to eat.

BOTTOM
Truly, a peck of provender. I could munch your good dry oats.
Methinks I have a great desire to a bottle of hay. Good hay, sweet
hay, hath no fellow.

TITANIA
I have a venturous fairy that shall seek   30
The squirrel's hoard, and fetch thee new nuts.

BOTTOM
I had rather have a handful or two of dried peas. But, I pray you,
let none of your people stir me; I have an exposition of sleep come
upon me.

tracks 35-37

36: **all ways:** in all directions

37: **woodbine:** a climbing plant

42–80:
David Harewood as Oberon, Adjoa Andoh as Titania, Richard McCabe as Puck
Michael Maloney as Oberon, Sarah Woodward as Titania, Ian Hughes as Puck

42: **dotage:** doting

Line 41: "Welcome, good Robin. See'st thou this sweet sight?": Stanley Tucci as Puck and Rupert Everett as Oberon in Michael Hoffman's 1999 production
Courtesy: Douglas Lanier

44: **sweet favors:** gifts or tokens of love

48: **sometime:** used to be

49: **orient:** lustrous

50: **flowerets:** tiny flowers

61: **other:** others

62: **repair:** go, travel

63: **accidents:** events

TITANIA

    Sleep thou, and I will wind thee in my arms.   35
    Fairies, begone, and be all ways away.

                                            Exit fairies

    So doth the woodbine the sweet honeysuckle
    Gently entwist; the female ivy so
    Enrings the barky fingers of the elm.
    O, how I love thee! How I dote on thee!   40
                 BOTTOM and TITANIA sleep
                          Enter PUCK

OBERON

    Welcome, good Robin. See'st thou this sweet sight?
    Her dotage now I do begin to pity.
    For, meeting her of late behind the wood,
    Seeking sweet favors from this hateful fool,
    I did upbraid her and fall out with her.   45
    For she his hairy temples then had rounded
    With a coronet of fresh and fragrant flowers;
    And that same dew, which sometime on the buds
    Was wont to swell like round and orient pearls,
    Stood now within the pretty flowerets' eyes   50
    Like tears that did their own disgrace bewail.
    When I had at my pleasure taunted her
    And she in mild terms begged my patience,
    I then did ask of her her changeling child,
    Which straight she gave me, and her fairy sent   55
    To bear him to my bower in fairyland.
    And now I have the boy, I will undo
    This hateful imperfection of her eyes.
    And, gentle Puck, take this transformèd scalp
    From off the head of this Athenian swain,   60
    That, he awaking when the other do,
    May all to Athens back again repair
    And think no more of this night's accidents
    But as the fierce vexation of a dream.
    But first I will release the fairy queen.   65
             [Squeezing the nectar on her eyelids]

42–80:
David Harewood as Oberon, Adjoa Andoh as Titania, Richard McCabe as Puck
Michael Maloney as Oberon, Sarah Woodward as Titania, Ian Hughes as Puck

Lines 66–69: "Be as thou wast wont to be; / See as thou wast wont to see: / Dian's bud o'er Cupid's flower / hath such force and blessèd power": Victor Jory as Oberon, James Cagney as Bottom, and Anita Louise as Titania in Dieterle/ Reinhardt's 1935 production

Courtesy: Douglas Lanier

66: **wont to:** used to

68: **Dian's bud:** the antidote to Oberon's magic flower, love-in-idleness, mentioned by Oberon in 3.2

77: **all these five:** the four lovers and Bottom

78: **charmeth:** acts like a magic spell

83: **solemnly:** ceremoniously

84: **triumphantly:** in a festive manner (a "triumph" was a public festival)

Be as thou wast wont to be;
See as thou wast wont to see:
Dian's bud o'er Cupid's flower
Hath such force and blessèd power.
Now, my Titania, wake you, my sweet queen.   70

TITANIA [*waking up*]
My Oberon! What visions have I seen!
Methought I was enamored of an ass.

OBERON
There lies your love.

TITANIA
                            How came these things to pass?
O, how mine eyes do loathe his visage now!

OBERON
Silence awhile. Robin, take off this head.   75
Titania, music call; and strike more dead
Than common sleep of all these five the sense.

TITANIA
Music, ho! Music, such as charmeth sleep!

                                                      Music

PUCK
Now, when thou wak'st, with thine own fool's eyes peep.

OBERON
Sound, music! Come, my queen, take hands with me,   80
And rock the ground whereon these sleepers be.
Now thou and I are new in amity,
And will tomorrow midnight solemnly
Dance in Duke Theseus' house triumphantly,
And bless it to all fair prosperity.   85
There shall the pairs of faithful lovers be
Wedded, with Theseus, all in jollity.

90: **sad:** solemn

92: **compass:** encircle, encompass

99: **our observation:** (of May Day, see note 1.1.163)

100: **we have the vaward of the day:** i.e., it is early yet (vaward = vanguard)

101: **music of my hounds:** sound of a pack of hounds pursuing prey

102: **uncouple:** set free for the hunt

Line 104: "We will, fair queen, up to the mountain's top": Theseus and Hippolyta
in Jiri Trnka's 1961 production
Courtesy: Douglas Lanier

107: **Cadmus:** mythical founder of Thebes

108: **bayed:** brought to bay (describing an animal cornered by hunters or other
predators)

109: **hounds of Sparta:** a legendary breed of hunting dogs

110: **chiding:** yelping

PUCK

 Fairy king, attend, and mark.
 I do hear the morning lark.

OBERON

 Then, my queen, in silence sad,   90
 Trip we after the night's shade.
 We the globe can compass soon,
 Swifter than the wandering moon.

TITANIA

 Come, my lord, and in our flight
 Tell me how it came this night   95
 That I sleeping here was found
 With these mortals on the ground.

           Exit All
        Horns playing within
  Enter THESEUS, HIPPOLYTA, EGEUS, and train

THESEUS

 Go, one of you, find out the forester;
 For now our observation is performed,
 And since we have the vaward of the day, 100
 My love shall hear the music of my hounds.
 Uncouple in the western valley; let them go!
 Dispatch, I say, and find the forester.

        Exit an Attendant

 We will, fair queen, up to the mountain's top,
 And mark the musical confusion   105
 Of hounds and echo in conjunction.

HIPPOLYTA

 I was with Hercules and Cadmus once,
 When in a wood of Crete they bayed the bear
 With hounds of Sparta. Never did I hear
 Such gallant chiding, for, besides the groves, 110
 The skies, the fountains, every region near
 Seemed all one mutual cry. I never heard
 So musical a discord, such sweet thunder.

115: **so flewed:** with large folds about the cheeks, like Spartan hounds

115: **sanded:** sandy, a light tan color

117: **dew-lapped:** with hanging folds of skin under the neck

117: **Thessalian:** bulls from Thessaly in Greece

118: **matched in mouth like bells:** bells that are graduated in melody from treble to bass in order to form a harmonious whole

119: **each under each:** (continuing the previous simile) like the notes on a scale

119: **cry:** the baying of a pack of hounds

119: **tuneable:** melodious

120: **holloed:** (hunting call)

120: **cheered:** encouraged

122: **soft:** gently

Line 122: "But, soft! What nymphs are these?": Theseus and Hippolyta come upon the sleeping lovers in Jiri Trnka's 1961 production

Courtesy: Douglas Lanier

126: **of:** at

128: **The rite of May:** May Day (see note 1.1.163)

129: **grace our solemnity:** in honor of our wedding ceremony

134–35: **Saint Valentine . . . couple now:** birds proverbially chose their mates on St. Valentine's Day

THESEUS
    My hounds are bred out of the Spartan kind,
    So flewed, so sanded, and their heads are hung   115
    With ears that sweep away the morning dew;
    Crook-kneeed, and dew-lapped like Thessalian bulls;
    Slow in pursuit, but matched in mouth like bells,
    Each under each. A cry more tuneable
    Was never holloed to, nor cheered with horn,   120
    In Crete, in Sparta, nor in Thessaly.
    Judge when you hear. But, soft! What nymphs are these?

EGEUS
    My lord, this is my daughter here asleep;
    And this, Lysander; this Demetrius is;
    This Helena, old Nedar's Helena.   125
    I wonder of their being here together.

THESEUS
    No doubt they rose up early to observe
    The rite of May, and hearing our intent,
    Came here in grace our solemnity.
    But speak, Egeus. Is not this the day   130
    That Hermia should give answer of her choice?

EGEUS
    It is, my lord.

THESEUS
    Go, bid the huntsmen wake them with their horns.
                                Horns and shout within
          LYSANDER, DEMETRIUS, HELENA, and HERMIA wake up
    Good morrow, friends. Saint Valentine is past.
    Begin these woodbirds but to couple now?   135

LYSANDER
    Pardon, my lord.

tracks 38-40

41–88:
Rupert Penry-Jones as Lysander, Clarence Smith as Demetrius, Paul Shelley
as Theseus, Amanda Root as Hermia, Saskia Wickham as Helena
Benjamin Soames as Lysander, David Timson as Egeus, Jamie Glover as
Demetrius, Jack Ellis as Theseus, Cathy Sara as Hermia, Emily Raymond as Helena

141: **amazèdly:** in bewilderment, as if lost in a maze

143: **truly:** truthfully

145: **bethink me:** recollect

148: **without:** outside

156: **hither:** in going

157: **hither:** here

158: **in fancy:** driven by love

159: **wot:** know

162: **an idle gaud:** a worthless trinket

THESEUS

               I pray you all, stand up.
I know you two are rival enemies.
How comes this gentle concord in the world,
That hatred is so far from jealousy,
To sleep by hate and fear no enmity?   140

LYSANDER

My lord, I shall reply amazèdly,
Half sleep, half waking. But as yet, I swear,
I cannot truly say how I came here;
But, as I think—for truly would I speak,
And now do I bethink me, so it is—   145
I came with Hermia hither. Our intent
Was to be gone from Athens, where we might,
Without the peril of the Athenian law—

EGEUS

Enough, enough, my lord! You have enough.
I beg the law, the law, upon his head.   150
They would have stolen away. They would, Demetrius,
Thereby to have defeated you and me:
You of your wife and me of my consent,
Of my consent that she should be your wife.

DEMETRIUS

My lord, fair Helen told me of their stealth,   155
Of this their purpose hither to this wood,
And I in fury hither followed them,
Fair Helena in fancy following me.
But, my good lord, I wot not by what power—
But by some power it is—my love to Hermia,   160
Melted as the snow, seems to me now
As the remembrance of an idle gaud
Which in my childhood I did dote upon,
And all the faith, the virtue of my heart,
The object and the pleasure of mine eye,   165
Is only Helena. To her, my lord,
Was I betrothed ere I saw Hermia.

tracks 38-40

41–88:
Rupert Penry-Jones as Lysander, Clarence Smith as Demetrius, Paul Shelley
as Theseus, Amanda Root as Hermia, Saskia Wickham as Helena
Benjamin Soames as Lysander, David Timson as Egeus, Jamie Glover as
Demetrius, Jack Ellis as Theseus, Cathy Sara as Hermia, Emily Raymond as Helena

168: **like in sickness:** like a sick person

174: **overbear:** overrule

177: **the morning now is something worn:** i.e., it is getting late
(something = somewhat)

180: **in great solemnity:** with an exquisitely beautiful and detailed ceremony

184: **parted:** divided, not quite focused

186–87: **like a jewel, mine own and not mine own:** something so precious
I can hardly believe it is mine

But, like in sickness, did I loathe this food;
But, as in health, come to my natural taste,
Now I do wish it, love it, long for it,   170
And will for evermore be true to it.

THESEUS
Fair lovers, you are fortunately met.
Of this discourse we more will hear anon.
Egeus, I will overbear your will,
For in the temple by and by with us   175
These couples shall eternally be knit,
And, for the morning now is something worn,
Our purposed hunting shall be set aside.
Away with us to Athens, three and three.
We'll hold a feast in great solemnity.   180
Come, Hippolyta.
                    Exit THESEUS, HIPPOLYTA, EGEUS, and train

DEMETRIUS
These things seem small and undistinguishable,
Like far-off mountains turnèd into clouds.

HERMIA
Methinks I see these things with parted eye,
When everything seems double.

HELENA
                        So methinks,   185
And I have found Demetrius like a jewel,
Mine own and not mine own.

DEMETRIUS
                        Are you sure
That we are awake? It seems to me
That yet we sleep, we dream. Do not you think
The duke was here, and bid us follow him?   190

HERMIA
Yea, and my father.

Scene: Hoffman's film makes the most of "Bottom's Dream" (as this soliloquy is often called) and of Kline's acting talents. Bottom wakes up thinking he had a beautiful dream until he notices the gift left to him by Titania: a tiny golden wreath, much like the fairy crown she wore when they were together. As Bottom delivers his lines, it becomes apparent that he is confused and uncertain. However, Hoffman grants him a lucid moment. Taking dramatic and romantic license at the end of the play, Hoffman has fairies—they could be golden fireflies—flit by Bottom in a swarm. Then, one hesitates, looks into Bottom's eyes, and flits away with the rest.

195: **my next:** my next line
197: **God's my life:** God save me

Line 198: "I have had a most rare vision": Kevin Kline as Bottom and Michelle Pfeiffer as Titania in Michael Hoffman's 1999 production
Corbis

200: **go about:** attempt
202: **patched fool:** wearing the motley (multicolored) suit of a fool (reinforces Puck's opinion of the foolishness of mortals)
203–05: **the eye of man . . . what my dream was:** Bottom misquotes Paul's letter, 1 Corinthians 2:9
206: **ballad:** a common song usually used to immortalize sensational stories and adventures
207: **it hath no bottom:** it can't ever be fully understood (also a pun on Bottom's experience—was he truly there or not?)
209: **gracious:** pleasing, wonderful
209: **her:** Thisbe's

HELENA

And Hippolyta.

LYSANDER

And he did bid us follow to the temple.

DEMETRIUS

Why, then, we are awake. Let's follow him,
And by the way let us recount our dreams.

Exit Lovers

BOTTOM [*Waking up*]

When my cue comes, call me, and I will answer. My next is, "Most   195
fair Pyramus." Heigh-ho! Peter Quince! Flute, the bellows-
mender! Snout, the tinker! Starveling! God's my life! Stolen
hence, and left me asleep? I have had a most rare vision. I have
had a dream, past the wit of man to say what dream it was. Man
is but an ass, if he go about to expound this dream. Methought I   200
was—there is no man can tell what. Methought I was—and
methought I had—but man is but a patched fool, if he will offer
to say what methought I had. The eye of man hath not heard, the
ear of man hath not seen, man's hand is not able to taste, his
tongue to conceive, nor his heart to report what my dream was. I   205
will get Peter Quince to write a ballad of this dream. It shall be
called "Bottom's Dream" because it hath no bottom, and I will
sing it in the latter end of a play, before the duke. Peradventure,
to make it the more gracious, I shall sing it at her death.

Exit

Costume for Snout from the 1948 staging directed by George Devine with sets and costumes by Margaret Harris

Rare Book and Special Collections Library, University of Illinois at Urbana-Champaign

Location: at Quince's house in Athens, though sometimes staged in a part of the village that stands outside of the palace—away from the Court

2: **out of doubt:** no doubt

2: **transported:** carried off by forest spirits

3: **marred:** ruined

5: **discharge:** perform

6: **wit:** intellect

7: **person:** appearance

9–10: **a thing of naught:** something shameful

12: **sport:** entertainment

13: **made men:** men with large fortunes

Enter QUINCE, FLUTE, SNOUT, and STARVELING

QUINCE
Have you sent to Bottom's house? Is he come home yet?

STARVELING
He cannot be heard of. Out of doubt he is transported.

FLUTE
If he come not, then the play is marred. It goes not forward, doth it?

QUINCE
It is not possible. You have not a man in all Athens able to discharge Pyramus but he.   5

FLUTE
No, he hath simply the best wit of any handicraft man in Athens.

QUINCE
Yea and the best person too, and he is a very paramour for a sweet voice.

FLUTE
You must say "paragon." A "paramour" is, God bless us, a thing of naught.   10
Enter SNUG

SNUG
Masters, the duke is coming from the temple, and there is two or three lords and ladies more married. If our sport had gone forward, we had all been made men.

Costume for Snug from the March 23, 1954 staging at the Shakespeare Memorial Theatre (Stratford-upon-Avon, England) directed by George Devine with sets and costumes by Margaret Harris

Rare Book and Special Collections Library, University of Illinois at Urbana-Champaign

15: **sixpence:** the standard yearly pension

18: **these hearts:** all my closest friends

20: **wonders:** amazing stories

21–22: **right as it fell out:** exactly as it happened

25: **strings:** (necessary to attach beards)

26: **ribbons to your pumps:** ribbons to adorn your shoes or pumps (light shoes for dancing)

28: **preferred:** selected for performance by the Master of the Revels, Philostrate, for performance at the Duke's wedding ceremonies

FLUTE

O sweet bully Bottom! Thus hath he lost sixpence a day during his
life; he could not have 'scaped sixpence a day. An the duke had not   15
given him sixpence a day for playing Pyramus, I'll be hanged. He
would have deserved it. Sixpence a day in Pyramus, or nothing.

Enter BOTTOM

BOTTOM

Where are these lads? Where are these hearts?

QUINCE

Bottom! O most courageous day! O most happy hour!

BOTTOM

Masters, I am to discourse wonders. But ask me not what, for if I   20
tell you, I am no true Athenian. I will tell you everything right as
it fell out.

QUINCE

Let us hear, sweet Bottom.

BOTTOM

Not a word of me. All that I will tell you is, that the duke hath
dined. Get your apparel together, good strings to your beards, new   25
ribbons to your pumps; meet presently at the palace; every man
look o'er his part; for the short and the long is, our play is
preferred. In any case, let Thisby have clean linen, and let not him
that plays the lion pare his nails, for they shall hang out for the
lion's claws. And, most dear actors, eat no onions nor garlic, for   30
we are to utter sweet breath, and I do not doubt but to hear them
say, it is a sweet comedy. No more words. Away! Go, away!

Exit All

[A Midsummer Night's Dream

Act 5

In the Palace of Theseus. From an early 20th century production.
Courtesy: Harry Rusche

Location: Theseus's palace in Athens where the Court is prepared for the wedding feast of Theseus and Hippolyta

1: **that:** the events
2: **may:** can
3: **antique:** old fashioned (also a pun on "antic," meaning "grotesque")
3: **fairy toys:** foolish tales, called "toys," about fairies
4: **seething brains:** i.e., active minds
5: **shaping fantasies:** imagination
5: **apprehend:** imagine
6: **comprehends:** understands
8: **all compact:** composed
11: **Helen:** referring to Helen of Troy (in Greek mythology, Helen is the most beautiful woman in the world)
20: **some bringer:** a source of
21: **fear:** object of fear
24: **transfigured so:** transformed and conjured
25: **more witnesseth than fancy's images:** something more than can be attributed to imagination
26: **constancy:** certainty
27: **howsoever:** in any case

Act 5, Scene 1]

Enter THESEUS, HIPPOLYTA, PHILOSTRATE,
Lords and Attendants

HIPPOLYTA
'Tis strange my Theseus, that these lovers speak of.

THESEUS
More strange than true. I never may believe
These antique fables, nor these fairy toys.
Lovers and madmen have such seething brains,
Such shaping fantasies, that apprehend   5
More than cool reason ever comprehends.
The lunatic, the lover and the poet
Are of imagination all compact.
One sees more devils than vast hell can hold:
That is, the madman. The lover, all as frantic,   10
Sees Helen's beauty in a brow of Egypt.
The poet's eye, in fine frenzy rolling,
Doth glance from heaven to earth, from earth to heaven;
And as imagination bodies forth
The forms of things unknown, the poet's pen   15
Turns them to shapes and gives to airy nothing
A local habitation and a name.
Such tricks hath strong imagination,
That if it would but apprehend some joy,
It comprehends some bringer of that joy;   20
Or in the night, imagining some fear,
How easy is a bush supposed a bear!

HIPPOLYTA
But all the story of the night told over,
And all their minds transfigured so together,
More witnesseth than fancy's images   25
And grows to something of great constancy,
But, howsoever, strange and admirable.

Lines 29–30: "Joy, gentle friends! Joy and fresh days of love / Accompany your hearts!"
Paul Whitthorne as Demetrius, Noel True as Hermia, Paris Remillard as Lysander, Kate
Nowlin as Helena, Lisa Tharps as Hippolyta and Mark H. Dold as Oberon in the
Shakespeare Theatre Company's 2003–04 production directed by Mark Lamos
Photo: Richard Termine

30: **more than:** i.e., more joy

31: **your board:** your table (for dining)

32: **masques:** courtly entertainments

34: **after-supper:** light course after the main meal

39: **abridgement:** pastime (to make the evening seem shorter)

42: **brief:** a short list

42: **ripe:** ready

44: **the battle with the Centaurs:** Referring to the battle between the Centaurs
and the Lapithae, an incident in the life of Hercules

47: **kinsman:** in Plutarch's *Life of Theseus*, Hercules and Theseus are related

49: **tearing the . . . their rage:** refers to the murder of Orpheus at the hands
of drunken women in the *Metamorphoses*

THESEUS

Here come the lovers, full of joy and mirth.
Enter LYSANDER, DEMETRIUS, HERMIA, and HELENA
Joy, gentle friends! Joy and fresh days of love
Accompany your hearts!

LYSANDER

More than to us   30
Wait in your royal walks, your board, your bed!

THESEUS

Come now; what masques, what dances shall we have,
To wear away this long age of three hours
Between our after-supper and bedtime?
Where is our usual manager of mirth?   35
What revels are in hand? Is there no play,
To ease the anguish of a torturing hour?
Call Philostrate.

PHILOSTRATE

Here, mighty Theseus.

THESEUS

Say, what abridgement have you for this evening?
What masque? What music? How shall we beguile   40
The lazy time, if not with some delight?

PHILOSTRATE

There is a brief how many sports are ripe.
Make choice of which your highness will see first.
Gives THESEUS a paper

THESEUS

"The battle with the Centaurs, to be sung
By an Athenian eunuch to the harp."   45
We'll none of that. That have I told my love,
In glory of my kinsman Hercules.
"The riot of the tipsy Bacchanals,
Tearing the Thracian singer in their rage."

50: **device:** entertainment

52: **thrice three Muses:** the nine muses of the arts, literature, and sciences

52–53: **the death . . . in beggary:** Spenser wrote of the neglect of learning and the destruction of the creative arts in *Teares of the Muses* (This could also be a possible reference to the untimely deaths of Kyd, Marlowe, and Greene between 1592–94; they all died in poverty and of questionable circumstances.)

55: **sorting with:** appropriate to

59: **hot ice and wondrous strange snow:** (provides a stark contrast—ice is not "hot" and snow is hardly "strange")

65: **fitted:** well cast for the role

70: **passion of loud laughter:** vehement laughter

72: **hard-handed:** with callused hands (from laboring)

74: **toiled:** taxed

74: **unbreathed:** unexercised

75: **against:** in preparation

That is an old device, and it was played   50
When I from Thebes came last a conqueror.
"The thrice three Muses mourning for the death
Of Learning, late deceased in beggary."
That is some satire, keen and critical,
Not sorting with a nuptial ceremony.   55
"A tedious brief scene of young Pyramus
And his love Thisbe; very tragical mirth."
Merry and tragical? Tedious and brief?
That is hot ice and wondrous strange snow.
How shall we find the concord of this discord?   60

PHILOSTRATE
A play there is, my lord, some ten words long—
Which is as brief as I have known a play—
But by ten words, my lord, it is too long,
Which makes it tedious; for in all the play
There is not one word apt, one player fitted.   65
And tragical, my noble lord, it is,
For Pyramus therein doth kill himself.
Which, when I saw rehearsed, I must confess,
Made mine eyes water; but more merry tears
The passion of loud laughter never shed.   70

THESEUS
What are they that do play it?

PHILOSTRATE
Hard-handed men that work in Athens here,
Which never labored in their minds till now,
And now have toiled their unbreathed memories
With this same play, against your nuptial.   75

THESEUS
And we will hear it.

PHILOSTRATE
                    No, my noble lord;
It is not for you. I have heard it over,
And it is nothing, nothing in the world,

80: **conned:** memorized

Costume for Philostrate from the 1948 staging directed by George Devine with sets and costumes by Margaret Harris
Rare Book and Special Collections Library, University of Illinois at Urbana-Champaign

85: **wretchedness o'ercharged:** simpletons (wretches) overburdened or overwhelmed by their tasks

88: **kind:** sort of thing

90: **take:** accept

92: **respect:** consideration

92: **takes it in might:** i.e., appreciates the effort

93: **clerks:** scholars

93: **purposèd:** intended

97: **throttle:** choke on

97: **practiced accent:** rehearsed speech

98: **dumbly have broke off:** abruptly stopped in silence

101: **fearful:** frightened

105: **to my capacity:** in my belief

Unless you can find sport in their intents,
Extremely stretched and conned with cruel pain   80
To do you service.

THESEUS
                    I will hear that play;
For never anything can be amiss
When simpleness and duty tender it.
Go, bring them in, and take your places, ladies.

Exit PHILOSTRATE

HIPPOLYTA
I love not to see wretchedness o'ercharged   85
And duty in his service perishing.

THESEUS
Why, gentle sweet, you shall see no such thing.

HIPPOLYTA
He says they can do nothing in this kind.

THESEUS
The kinder we, to give them thanks for nothing.
Our sport shall be to take what they mistake;   90
And what poor duty cannot do,
Noble respect, takes it in might, not merit.
Where I have come, great clerks have purposèd
To greet me with premeditated welcomes,
Where I have seen them shiver and look pale,   95
Make periods in the midst of sentences,
Throttle their practiced accent in their fears
And in conclusion dumbly have broke off,
Not paying me a welcome. Trust me, sweet,
Out of this silence yet I picked a welcome,   100
And in the modesty of fearful duty,
I read as much as from the rattling tongue
Of saucy and audacious eloquence.
Love, therefore, and tongue-tied simplicity
In least speak most, to my capacity.   105

Reenter PHILOSTRATE

106: **Prologue:** the Chorus who introduces and narrates the play
106: **addressed:** ready

Scene: In 1840, the famous Shakespearean actress Madame Lucia Bartolozzi Vestris produced *A Midsummer Night's Dream* at Covent Garden. Madame Vestris played the role of Oberon, dressed in a Grecian tunic. This nearly uncut version of Shakespeare's play was received with critical acclaim and influenced future Shakespearean productions, restoring many of the scenes (such as the Rude Mechanicals' play) that had been frequently cut from the play after the Restoration period.

tracks 41-43

108–117:
Richard Cordery as Quince
Bill Horsley as Quince

108: **if we offend:** foreshadowing Puck's speech in the Epilogue
111: **end:** purpose
113: **minding:** intending
118: **This fellow . . . upon points:** Like Bottom, Quince frequently misspeaks, mispronounces, and mispunctuates. Theseus comments on it by punning on the word "points," meaning "details" as well as "punctuation marks."
119: **rid:** ridden
119: **rough:** unbroken
119: **the stop:** 1) how to rein in a colt   2) the punctuation of the speech
121: **recorder:** a wind instrument like a flute
122: **in government:** controlled
123: **nothing:** not at all

Stage Direction: **Enter Pyramus . . . Snug:** The mechanicals' play opens with a standard Dumb Show. During the early years of English theatre, plays were often prefaced by an opening performance that anticipated the upcoming drama, preparing the audience for what was to come. A narrator, or "Prologue," would present the "Argument" and players would mime the narration. This was also a good way to introduce the characters.

PHILOSTRATE
So please your grace, the Prologue is addressed.

THESEUS
Let him approach.

A flourish of trumpets
Enter QUINCE

QUINCE *as Prologue*
If we offend, it is with our goodwill.
That you should think, we come not to offend,
But with goodwill. To show our simple skill,   110
That is the true beginning of our end.
Consider then we come but in despite.
We do not come as minding to content you,
Our true intent is. All for your delight
We are not here. That you should here repent you,   115
The actors are at hand and by their show,
You shall know all that you are like to know.

THESEUS
This fellow doth not stand upon points.

LYSANDER
He hath rid his prologue like a rough colt; he knows not the stop.
A good moral, my lord: it is not enough to speak, but to speak true.   120

HIPPOLYTA
Indeed he hath played on his prologue like a child on a recorder;
a sound, but not in government.

THESEUS
His speech was like a tangled chain, nothing impaired but all
disordered. Who is next?
Enter Pyramus (BOTTOM) and Thisbe (FLUTE), Wall (SNOUT),
Moonshine (STARVELING), and Lion (SNUG)

Scene: Although Reinhardt did not intend to cast the mechanicals with Hollywood movie stars, their early vaudevillian training and years spent as traveling players served this adaptation well. Cagney as Bottom playing Pyramus and Joe E. Brown as Flute playing Thisbe are magnificent. They overact, forget their lines, stammer nervously, and explain the action to the commenting audience without regard for the illusion they are trying to create in the play. They are oblivious to the question of illusion and cannot distinguish between playing their parts and speaking to the audience. The result is wonderful chaos.

Line 127: "This man is Pyramus, if you would know": The cast of the Shakespeare Theatre Company's 2003–04 production directed by Mark Lamos
Photo: Richard Termine

135: **no scorn:** no disgrace

137: **hight:** is called

140: **did fall:** dropped

142: **tall:** brave, courageous

145: **broached:** stabbed

148: **lovers twain:** lovers separated

149: **At large:** in full

QUINCE *as Prologue*

> *Gentles, perchance you wonder at this show;*   125
> *But wonder on, till truth make all things plain.*
> *This man is Pyramus, if you would know;*
> *This beauteous lady Thisby is certain.*
> *This man, with lime and rough-cast, doth present*
> *Wall, that vile Wall which did these lovers sunder;*   130
> *And through Wall's chink, poor souls, they are content*
> *To whisper, at the which let no man wonder.*
> *This man, with lanthorn, dog, and bush of thorn,*
> *Presenteth Moonshine; for, if you will know,*
> *By moonshine did these lovers think no scorn*   135
> *To meet at Ninus' tomb, there, there to woo.*
> *This grisly beast, which Lion hight by name,*
> *The trusty Thisby, coming first by night,*
> *Did scare away, or rather did affright;*
> *And, as she fled, her mantle she did fall,*   140
> *Which Lion vile with bloody mouth did stain.*
> *Anon comes Pyramus, sweet youth and tall,*
> *And finds his trusty Thisby's mantle slain.*
> *Whereat, with blade, with bloody blameful blade,*
> *He bravely broached is boiling bloody breast;*   145
> *And Thisby, tarrying in mulberry shade,*
> *His dagger drew, and died. For all the rest,*
> *Let Lion, Moonshine, Wall, and lovers twain*
> *At large discourse, while here they do remain.*
>
> *Exit all but Wall (SNOUT)*

THESEUS

I wonder if the lion be to speak.   150

DEMETRIUS

No wonder, my lord. One lion may, when many asses do.

160: **is, right and sinister:** goes from right to left (sinister)

162: **lime and hair:** i.e., the wall (these are the materials comprising roughcast)

163: **partition:** 1) section of a wall   2) formal term for part of a speech (oratory)

Scene: Bottom (Cagney) enters the stage rolling his r's dramatically, flourishing his obviously homemade sword. Wall, wearing a tabard painted in brick-and-mortar, carrying a brick, and laughing nervously, provides just the right touch for Cagney and Brown's comic duet. As Thisbe, Joe E. Brown wears a white dress stuffed with cloth for breasts and painted around the edge of the skirt with big, uneven hearts. The innuendos during the lovers talk and kiss through the "chink" in the Wall is frankly sexual but done so cleverly that it can only be funny. After the play, the epilogue (Arthur Treacher) reminds us that the magic of night is returning.

165: **grim-looked:** depressing

172: **eyne:** eyes

Stage Direction: *Wall holds up his fingers*: Brad Waller as Snug (background), David Sabin as Nick Bottom, Ryan Artzberger as Tom Snout, Greg Felden as Francis Flute, and John Livingstone Rolle as Robin Starveling in the Shakespeare Theatre Company's 2003–04 production directed by Mark Lamos
Photo: Richard Termine

176: **stones:** (a pun on testicles)

177: **sensible:** 1) capable of feeling   2) having good sense

177: **again:** in return

SNOUT *as Wall*

> *In this same interlude it doth befall*
> *That I, one Snout by name, present a wall;*
> *And such a wall, as I would have you think,*
> *That had in it a crannied hole or chink,*   155
> *Through which the lovers, Pyramus and Thisby,*
> *Did whisper often very secretly.*
> *This loam, this rough-cast and this stone doth show*
> *That I am that same wall. The truth is so.*
> *And this the cranny is, right and sinister,*   160
> *Through which the fearful lovers are to whisper.*

THESEUS

> Would you desire lime and hair to speak better?

DEMETRIUS

> It is the wittiest partition that ever I heard discourse, my lord.
>
> > *Enter Pyramus (BOTTOM)*

THESEUS

> Pyramus draws near the wall. Silence!

BOTTOM *as Pyramus*

> *O grim-looked night! O night with hue so black!*   165
> *O night, which ever art when day is not!*
> *O night, O night! Alack, alack, alack,*
> *I fear my Thisby's promise is forgot!*
> *And thou, O wall, O sweet, O lovely wall,*
> *That stand'st between her father's ground and mine!*   170
> *Thou wall, O wall, O sweet and lovely wall,*
> *Show me thy chink, to blink through with mine eyne!*
>
> > *Wall holds up his fingers*
>
> *Thanks, courteous wall. Jove shield thee well for this!*
> *But what see I? No Thisby do I see.*
> *O wicked wall, through whom I see no bliss!*   175
> *Cursed be thy stones for thus deceiving me!*

THESEUS

> The wall, methinks, being sensible, should curse again.

180: **fall pat:** happen exactly

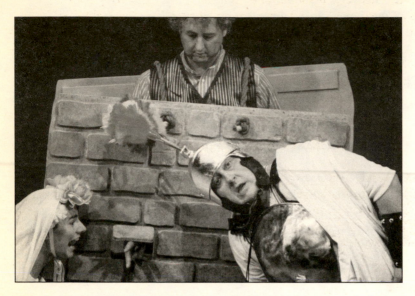

Line 185: "I see a voice! Now will I to the chink": Daniel Evans as Thisbe, Howard
Crossley as Wall, and Desmond Barrit as Pyramus in the 1994 Royal Shakespeare
Company production directed by Adrian Noble
Corbis

189: **Limander:** Bottom confuses the name of Leander who drowned while
swimming across the Hellespont to meet his love, Hero

190: **Helen:** Helen of Troy (Bottom is misspeaking; he means to say Hero,
the lover of Leander)

191: **Shafalus to Procrus:** Bottom means Cephalus and Procris, two other
famous lovers

BOTTOM
No, in truth, sir, he should not. "Deceiving me" is Thisby's cue.
She is to enter now, and I am to spy her through the wall. You
shall see, it will fall pat as I told you. Yonder she comes.   180

Enter Thisbe (FLUTE)

FLUTE *as Thisbe*
 O wall, full often hast thou heard my moans,
 For parting my fair Pyramus and me!
 My cherry lips have often kissed thy stones,
 Thy stones with lime and hair knit up in thee.

BOTTOM *as Pyramus*
 I see a voice! Now will I to the chink,   185
 To spy an I can hear my Thisby's face. Thisby? Thisby!

FLUTE *as Thisbe*
 My love! Thou art my love, I think.

BOTTOM *as Pyramus*
 Think what thou wilt, I am thy lover's grace;
 And, like Limander, am I trusty still.

FLUTE *as Thisbe*
 And I like Helen, till the Fates me kill.   190

BOTTOM *as Pyramus*
 Not Shafalus to Procrus was so true.

FLUTE *as Thisbe*
 As Shafalus to Procrus, I to you.

BOTTOM *as Pyramus*
 O kiss me through the hole of this vile wall!

FLUTE *as Thisbe*
 I kiss the wall's hole, not your lips at all.

BOTTOM *as Pyramus*
 Wilt thou at Ninny's tomb meet me straightway?   195

196: **'tide:** (betide) come

Costume for Snout as Wall from the 1948 staging directed by George Devine with sets and costumes by Margaret Harris

200: **wilful:** willing

200–201: **without warning:** without warning the parents (also a proverbial reference to "the walls have ears")

203–04: **The best . . . amend them:** in these two lines, Theseus is referring to actors, the best of whom (he says) are mere imitations, without substance (shadows)

203: **in this kind:** of this sort

203: **shadows:** likenesses

213–14: **I, one Snug the joiner . . . no lion's dam:** I'm pretending to be a fierce lion but, in reality, I'm just Snug, the joiner

214: **fell:** fierce

214: **dam:** mother

FLUTE *as Thisbe*
>   *'Tide life, 'tide death, I come without delay.*
>   *Exit Pyramus (BOTTOM) and Thisbe (FLUTE)*

SNOUT *as Wall*
>   *Thus have I, Wall, my part dischargèd so;*
>   *And, being done, thus Wall away doth go.*

>   *Exit*

THESEUS
Now is the wall down between the two neighbors.

DEMETRIUS
No remedy, my lord, when walls are so wilful to hear without   200
warning.

HIPPOLYTA
This is the silliest stuff that ever I heard.

THESEUS
The best in this kind are but shadows; and the worst are no worse, if
imagination amend them.

HIPPOLYTA
It must be your imagination then, and not theirs.   205

THESEUS
If we imagine no worse of them than they of themselves, they may
pass for excellent men. Here come two noble beasts in, a man and
a lion.
>   *Enter Lion (SNUG) and Moonshine (STARVELING)*

SNUG *as Lion*
>   *You, ladies, you, whose gentle hearts do fear*
>   *The smallest monstrous mouse that creeps on floor,*   210
>   *May now perchance both quake and tremble here,*
>   *When lion rough in wildest rage doth roar.*
>   *Then know that I, one Snug the joiner, am*
>   *A lion fell, nor else no lion's dam;*
>   *For, if I should as lion come in strife*   215
>   *Into this place, 'twere pity on my life.*

219: a very fox for his valor: i.e., his valor consists of being sly and crafty

220: a goose for his discretion: i.e., foolish and indiscrete

226: hornèd moon: crescent moon

Costume for Starveling as Moonshine from the March 23, 1954 staging at the
Shakespeare Memorial Theatre (Stratford-upon-Avon, England) directed by George
Devine with sets and costumes by Margaret Harris
Rare Book and Special Collections Library, University of Illinois at Urbana-Champaign

227: horns on his head: signifies a cuckold, a man whose wife is unfaithful

228: crescent: waxing moon

THESEUS
A very gentle beast, of a good conscience.

DEMETRIUS
The very best at a beast, my lord, that e'er I saw.

LYSANDER
This lion is a very fox for his valor.

THESEUS
True, and a goose for his discretion.   220

DEMETRIUS
Not so, my lord, for his valor cannot carry his discretion, and the fox carries the goose.

THESEUS
His discretion, I am sure, cannot carry his valor, for the goose carries not the fox. It is well. Leave it to his discretion, and let us listen to the moon.   225

STARVELING *as Moonshine*
        This lanthorn doth the hornèd moon present—

DEMETRIUS
He should have worn the horns on his head.

THESEUS
He is no crescent, and his horns are invisible within the circumference.

STARVELING *as Moonshine*
        This lanthorn doth the hornèd moon present;   230
        Myself the man i' th' moon do seem to be.

THESEUS
This is the greatest error of all the rest; the man should be put into the lantern. How is it else "the man i' th' moon?"

234: **for the candle:** for fear of the candle

235: **in snuff:** 1) angry   2) in need of being snuffed

238: **stay:** wait for

Costume for Flute as Thisbe from the March 23, 1954 staging at the Shakespeare
Memorial Theatre (Stratford-upon-Avon, England) directed by George Devine
with sets and costumes by Margaret Harris
Rare Book and Special Collections Library, University of Illinois at Urbana-Champaign

DEMETRIUS
He dares not come there for the candle; for you see, it is already
in snuff.   235

HIPPOLYTA
I am aweary of this moon. Would he would change!

THESEUS
It appears, by his small light of discretion, that he is in the wane;
but yet, in courtesy, in all reason, we must stay the time.

LYSANDER
Proceed, Moon.

STARVELING
All that I have to say is to tell you that the lanthorn is the moon;   240
I, the man in the moon; this thorn-bush, my thorn-bush; and this
dog, my dog.

DEMETRIUS
Why, all these should be in the lantern, for all these are in the
moon. But, silence! Here comes Thisbe.

Enter Thisbe (FLUTE)

FLUTE *as Thisbe*
   This is old Ninny's tomb. Where is my love?   245

SNUG *as Lion*
   O!

Lion roars and Thisbe runs away

DEMETRIUS
Well roared, Lion.

THESEUS
Well run, Thisbe.

HIPPOLYTA
Well shone, Moon. Truly, the moon shines with a good grace.

Lion shakes Thisbe's mantle

250: **well moused:** shaken, torn

Line 253: "Sweet Moon, I thank thee for thy sunny beams": F. Murray Abraham as Bottom with Ensemble in the Public Theater's 1987-88 production directed by A. J. Antoon

Photo: George E. Joseph

259: **dole:** sad event (dolorous)
265: **Furies:** avenging goddesses of Greek mythology
265: **fell:** savage, fierce
266: **Fates:** the three goddesses of Greek myth (Clotho, Lachesis, and Atropos) who spin, draw, and cut the thread of human life
267: **cut thread and thrum:** i.e., control the thread of life
267: **thrum:** unwoven end of a thread
268: **quail:** overpower
268: **quell:** kill, destroy
269–70: **this passion . . . look sad:** There are reasons to be sad (e.g., the death of a dear friend), but this portrayal of passion is not one of them
271: **beshrew:** curse
272: **wherefore:** why
272: **frame:** create
273: **deflowered:** ruined, as in lost virginity; Bottom means to say "devoured"

THESEUS
Well moused, Lion.   250

LYSANDER
And so the lion vanished.

Exit Lion (SNUG)
Enter Pyramus (BOTTOM)

DEMETRIUS
And then came Pyramus.

BOTTOM *as Pyramus*
> *Sweet Moon, I thank thee for thy sunny beams;*
> *I thank thee, Moon, for shining now so bright;*
> *For, by thy gracious, golden, glittering gleams,*   255
> *I trust to take of truest Thisby sight.*
> *But stay, O spite!*
> *But mark, poor knight,*
> *What dreadful dole is here!*
> *Eyes, do you see?*   260
> *How can it be?*
> *O dainty duck! O dear!*
> *Thy mantle good,*
> *What, stained with blood!*
> *Approach, ye Furies fell!*   265
> *O Fates, come, come,*
> *Cut thread and thrum;*
> *Quail, crush, conclude, and quell!*

THESEUS
This passion, and the death of a dear friend, would go near to
make a man look sad.   270

HIPPOLYTA
Beshrew my heart, but I pity the man.

BOTTOM *as Pyramus*
> *O wherefore, Nature, didst thou lions frame?*
> *Since lion vile hath here deflowered my dear,*

278: **pap:** breast

288: **ace:** pun on die—one of a pair of dice and the side of the die with one spot; also, the lowest throw in the game

288: **one:** unique

290: **ass:** a pun on ace as well as on the character of Bottom and his transformation

291: **how chance Moonshine is gone:** why has Moonshine left

293: **passion:** passionate speech

Costume for Pyramus from the 1948 staging directed by George Devine with sets and costumes by Margaret Harris
Rare Book and Special Collections Library, University of Illinois at Urbana-Champaign

Which is—no, no—which was the fairest dame
That lived, that loved, that liked, that looked with cheer?   275
Come, tears, confound;
Out, sword, and wound
The pap of Pyramus;
Ay, that left pap,
Where heart doth hop.   280

> *Stabs himself*

Thus die I, thus, thus, thus.
Now am I dead,
Now am I fled;
My soul is in the sky.
Tongue, lose thy light;   285
Moon take thy flight.

> *Exit Moonshine (STARVELING)*

Now die, die, die, die, die!

> *Pyramus dies*

DEMETRIUS
No die, but an ace, for him, for he is but one.

LYSANDER
Less than an ace, man, for he is dead; he is nothing.

THESEUS
With the help of a surgeon he might yet recover and prove an ass.   290

HIPPOLYTA
How chance Moonshine is gone before Thisbe comes back and finds her lover?

THESEUS
She will find him by starlight. Here she comes, and her passion ends the play.

> *Reenter Thisbe (FLUTE)*

HIPPOLYTA
Methinks she should not use a long one for such a Pyramus.   295
I hope she will be brief.

297: **mote:** a small particle (and one of Titania's attendants)

297: **which Pyramus, which Thisbe:** whether Pyramus or Thisbe

301: **means:** moans

301: **videlicet:** Latin for "to wit"

Line 303: "What, dead, my dove?": Brad Waller as Snug, David Sabin as Nick Bottom, and Greg Felden as Francis Flute in the Shakespeare Theatre Company's 2003–04 production directed by Mark Lamos
Photo: Richard Termine

305: **dumb:** mute

314: **Sisters Three:** the Fates

318: **shore:** shorn, cut

319: **his thread of silk:** i.e., thread of his life ("silk" rhymes with a previous word, "milk")

322: **imbrue:** stain with blood

DEMETRIUS
    A mote will turn the balance, which Pyramus, which Thisbe, is
    the better; he for a man, God warrant us; she for a woman, God
    bless us.

LYSANDER
    She hath spied him already with those sweet eyes.   300

DEMETRIUS
    And thus she means, *videlicet*—

FLUTE *as Thisbe*
        Asleep, my love?
        What, dead, my dove?
        O Pyramus, arise!
        Speak, speak. Quite dumb?   305
        Dead, dead? A tomb
        Must cover thy sweet eyes.
        These lily lips,
        This cherry nose,
        These yellow cowslip cheeks,   310
        Are gone, are gone!
        Lovers, make moan;
        His eyes were green as leeks.
        O Sisters Three,
        Come, come to me   315
        With hands as pale as milk;
        Lay them in gore,
        Since you have shore
        With shears his thread of silk.
        Tongue, not a word!   320
        Come, trusty sword,
        Come, blade, my breast imbrue!
                                    Stabs herself

        And, farewell, friends;
        Thus Thisby ends.
        Adieu, adieu, adieu.   325
                                    Thisbe dies

329: **Bergomask dance:** rustic Venetian dance

Stage Direction: *Dance begins*: The ensemble at the end of Pyramus and Thisbe in Dieterle/Reinhardt's 1935 production
Courtesy: Douglas Lanier

337: **iron tongue:** the clapper of a bell

337: **told:** counted, chimed

338: **fairy time:** between midnight and dawn

339: **outsleep:** oversleep

340: **overwatched:** stayed up too late

341: **palpable-gross:** obviously crude

343: **fortnight:** two weeks

THESEUS

Moonshine and Lion are left to bury the dead.

DEMETRIUS

Ay, and Wall too.

BOTTOM sits up

BOTTOM

No, I assure you; the wall is down that parted their fathers. Will
it please you to see the epilogue, or to hear a Bergomask dance
between two of our company?   330

THESEUS

No epilogue, I pray you. For your play needs no excuse. Never
excuse; for when the players are all dead, there needs none to be
blamed. Marry, if he that writ it had played Pyramus and hanged
himself in Thisbe's garter, it would have been a fine tragedy; and
so it is, truly, and very notably discharged. But come, your Bergo-   335
mask. Let your epilogue alone.

Dance begins
Exit players

The iron tongue of midnight hath told twelve.
Lovers, to bed; 'tis almost fairy time.
I fear we shall outsleep the coming morn
As much as we this night have overwatched.   340
This palpable-gross play hath well beguiled
The heavy gait of night. Sweet friends, to bed.
A fortnight hold we this solemnity
In nightly revels and new jollity.

Exit

Location: Theseus's palace at midnight. All are gone to bed and now the fairies are awake. Puck, as Robin Goodfellow, enters carrying his trademark broom.

3: **heavy ploughman:** weary farmer

4: **fordone:** exhausted

5: **wasted brands:** burned-out logs

7–8: **puts the wretch that lies in woe in remembrance:** reminds the wretch that lies in woe

11: **every one lets forth his sprite:** every grave releases the ghost that sleeps there

14: **triple Hecate's team:** Hecate ruled as Luna (or Cynthis) in the heavens, Diana on earth, and Prosperina in Hades.

17: **frolic:** merry

Scene: Hoffman's Puck now wears human clothing, with a hat to cover his goblin horns and a broom to emphasize his role in English folklore.

20: **behind:** sweeping the dust behind the door or under the rug (This is a reference to Robin Goodfellow, who helped industrious housemaids but played tricks on lazy ones.)

Act 5, Scene 2]

Enter PUCK, carrying the trademark broom
of ROBIN GOODFELLOW

PUCK

 Now the hungry lion roars,
 And the wolf behowls the moon;
 Whilst the heavy ploughman snores,
 All with weary task fordone.
 Now the wasted brands do glow,   5
 Whilst the screech-owl, screeching loud,
 Puts the wretch that lies in woe
 In remembrance of a shroud.
 Now it is the time of night
 That the graves all gaping wide,   10
 Every one lets forth his sprite,
 In the church-way paths to glide.
 And we fairies, that do run
 By the triple Hecate's team,
 From the presence of the sun,   15
 Following darkness like a dream,
 Now are frolic. Not a mouse
 Shall disturb this hallowed house.
 I am sent with broom before,
 To sweep the dust behind the door.   20

Enter OBERON and TITANIA with their train

OBERON

 Through the house give gathering light,
 By the dead and drowsy fire.
 Every elf and fairy sprite
 Hop as light as bird from brier;
 And this ditty, after me,   25
 Sing, and dance it trippingly.

27: **rehearse:** recite

Scene: These lines are not assigned to Oberon in the First Folio; however, it is frequently staged this way

Line 33: "To the best bride-bed will we": Rupert Everett as Oberon and Michelle Pfeiffer as Titania in Michael Hoffman's 1999 production
Courtesy: Douglas Lanier

35: **issue:** children

35: **create:** created

39: **blots of Nature's hands:** i.e., abnormalities

40: **in their issue stand:** appear in their children (issue)

42: **mark prodigious:** any unnatural mark

45: **consecrate:** to bless (as in the old Catholic custom of blessing the marriage bed with Holy Water)

47: **several:** separate

TITANIA
    First, rehearse your song by rote,
    To each word a warbling note.
    Hand in hand, with fairy grace,
    Will we sing and bless this place.   30
               Oberon leads the singing

OBERON
      Now, until the break of day,
      Through this house each fairy stray.
      To the best bride-bed will we,
      Which by us shall blessèd be;
      And the issue there create   35
      Ever shall be fortunate.
      So shall all the couples three
      Ever true in loving be;
      And the blots of Nature's hand
      Shall not in their issue stand;   40
      Never mole, hare lip, nor scar,
      Nor mark prodigious, such as are
      Despisèd in nativity,
      Shall upon their children be.
      With this field-dew consecrate,   45
      Every fairy take his gait;
      And each several chamber bless,
      Through this palace, with sweet peace;
      And the owner of it blest
      Ever shall in safety rest.   50
      Trip away; make no stay;
      Meet me all by break of day.
           Exit OBERON, TITANIA, and train,
               leaving only PUCK behind

tracks 44–46

1–16:
Richard McCabe as Puck
Annette Crosbie as Puck

Randy Reyes as Puck in the 1999–2000 production at the Guthrie Theater
directed by Joe Dowling
Photo: Michal Daniel

1: **shadows:** actors, illusionists
5: **idle:** trivial
7: **reprehend:** rebuke
8: **we will mend:** we will improve next time
11: **serpent's tongue:** hissing, a clear reference to an unsatisfied or disappointed audience
15: **give me your hands, if we be friends:** please applaud if you enjoyed our play
16: **restore amends:** I'll give you something good in return (his mischievous and interfering nature continues even as the play ends)

Scene: In Reinhardt's film, Rooney as Puck is nearly transparent (a radical new cinematic technique at the time) as he begs the audience to show their appreciation. But we get the feeling that he doesn't really care as he disappears with the moonlight, a moonlight that he laughingly extinguishes with a quick blow. In Hoffman's farewell scene, Puck looks on as Bottom muses about his fairy dream. Then cap in hand, he addresses the audience and asks them for their hands. He walks off into the night, securing his hat and swinging his mischievous broom over his shoulder.

Epilogue

PUCK
    If we shadows have offended,
    Think but this, and all is mended:
    That you have but slumbered here
    While these visions did appear.
    And this weak and idle theme,   5
    No more yielding but a dream,
    Gentles, do not reprehend.
    If you pardon, we will mend.
    And, as I am an honest Puck,
    If we have unearnèd luck   10
    Now to 'scape the serpent's tongue,
    We will make amends ere long;
    Else the Puck a liar call.
    So, good night unto you all.
    Give me your hands, if we be friends,   15
    And Robin shall restore amends.

Exit

The Cast Speaks

THE 2003–04 CAST FROM THE SHAKESPEARE THEATRE
COMPANY IN WASHINGTON, DC

Marie Macaisa

In the text of a play, directors, actors, and other interpreters of Shakespeare's work find a wealth of information. In *A Midsummer Night's Dream*, we are presented with quite a few examples of the many facets of love. There are the young lovers, Lysander and Hermia, initially determined to be together; there is the duke, Theseus, who wooed and won his bride-to-be, Hippolyta, in battle; and the king and queen of the fairies, Oberon and Titania, whose lovers' quarrel is so powerful it has upended the natural world. There is Bottom the Weaver, turned into an ass and loved by Titania while under Puck's spell; and finally, the other set of young lovers, Helena and Demetrius, who eventually get married but only after Demetrius has been anointed with love juice. Just what are we to make of these couples? Who is really in love?

While providing extra information, Shakespeare (like all playwrights and unlike novelists) also leaves gaps. We are thus coaxed to fill in the missing information ourselves, either through reasonable surmises (we can guess that Oberon was probably jealous of the attention Titania was paying her changeling boy) or through backstories we supply on our own (the idea that Egeus was grieving for his wife, not present in the text, to explain his harsh attitude towards his daughter). This mix of simultaneously knowing too much and not enough enables us to paint varied vivid interpretations of a single play.

In staging a play, directors create a vision for their production, starting from the text but also moving beyond that by making decisions on what isn't in the text. In collaboration with actors, they flesh out the characters: they create stories that explain their actions, they determine motivations, and they speculate on the nature of their relationships. Shakespeare directors have rich texts to draw on and hundreds of years of performances for inspiration. Thus we, the audience, can experience the same play anew each time we see a different production of it: perhaps it is in an unfamiliar setting, perhaps it is in a scene or characterization we hadn't noticed in the past, perhaps it is in the realization that we have changed our opinions about the actions of the characters in the play. Whatever the case, a closer look into one cast's interpretation creates an opportunity for us to make up our own minds about their stories and in the process, gain new insights not just into a play hundreds of years old, but quite possibly, into ourselves.

THE SHAKESPEARE THEATRE COMPANY, WASHINGTON, DC, 2003–04

"It's a near perfect play, as you all know," says director Mark Lamos of *A Midsummer Night's Dream.* "It's a play in which you can feel a vibrant young playwright experimenting with plot, verse, comedy, and this amazingly resonant idea of the subconscious—long before Freud." The central idea of Lamos's production is that dreams are "skeins woven out of our subconscious and out of the real life we live, surrounding us like a cocoon." He thus envelops the play in imagination. His conceit for the play is that all the events occur in a little boy's mind, but not just any little boy; in fact, he is Hippolyta's son, who was having trouble adjusting to his new father-to-be, Theseus. It's not hard to imagine how difficult it must have been for the boy during the "courtship." Theseus himself reminds Hippolyta that she was wooed and won on the battlefield: "I wooed thee with my sword / And won thy love doing thee injuries"

This production opens with the boy silently playing and making shadow puppets (which later on become images in the forest). Philostrate enters and turns on the lights, thus rudely ending his playtime. Hippolyta then walks onstage and the play begins. This conceit frames the doubling nicely. Theseus and Hippolyta later become Oberon and Titania while the boy is the changeling. They enter fighting, reflecting the strife in the family. Ironically, the boy who appears to be a helpless object of a custody battle is in fact in control.

These interviews were conducted in January 2006, six months after the revival of the original production. The actors were interviewed individually and asked about their characters, their relationships, and a scene or two in which their character is key. Keep in mind that their answers represent but one interpretation of the play. You may be surprised, you may agree or disagree strongly with a point of view. That is exactly the point.

Hippolyta (Lisa Tharps), Theseus (Mark H. Dold), the Changeling Boy (James Bonilla) and Philostrate (Daniel Breaker) in the added scene before Act 1.
Photo: Richard Termine

The play opens with Egeus, father of Hermia, demanding justice from the Duke. His daughter has refused to marry his choice of husband, Demetrius, because she is in love with Lysander.

Egeus: Edward Gero

I imagined, although it's not in the text, that Hermia's mother died when she was very young, and that I've raised her on my own. She's definitely her father's daughter, stubborn like I am.

I played Egeus as a comic figure, with over-the-top outrage. I don't think he means for her to be put to death if she disobeys him, but he is exercising what little control he has over her.

Because we were doubling (I also played Peter Quince), Egeus is only in one other scene, the one when the lovers awaken [4.1]. He's still in the same place as his other scene, begging Theseus to punish Lysander. When he is overruled, he is surprised and leaves in a daze. He wanders around the forest and gets lost.

Theseus, the duke of Athens, attempts a compromise between father and daughter. Instead of forcing Hermia to marry someone she does not love or putting her to death, he presents her the option of living forever chastely. This Solomonic judgment, as well as his treatment of the Mechanicals later in the play, paints a certain picture of Theseus's character. Indeed, his portrayal starts from these behaviors. It is hard to reconcile this Theseus with the one who won his fiancée on the battlefield while doing her injuries.

Theseus: Mark H. Dold

He seems to be a very dry, officious person. I tried to make him a nerd, very bookish but trying to be cool. I wanted to give him a little charm. He's with Hippolyta, who's a remarkable warrior, but nothing in his own language indicates that he is her equal, other than his mentioning that he conquered and won her in battle. Most of the time he is in control, but he is a little taken aback by his feelings for her. Otherwise, he speaks intelligently, behaves rationally, and tries to do the right thing. When he is presented with two unacceptable choices—force Hermia to marry against her will or put her to death—he comes up with the compromise "to abjure forever the society of men." The way he treats the Mechanicals is very telling of his character. He appreciates them for their efforts and he respects them.

Hippolyta: Lisa Tharps

Hippolyta is a brave warrior woman, queen of the Amazons. But where she is, that doesn't seem to matter. Theseus says he won her in battle, "doing thee injuries." She has suffered a great loss and is totally out of her element.

She's in a strange position. She loves Theseus, yet he has also destroyed the life she knew. I'm not sure how she reconciles this, except with her silence. She doesn't speak much, and I think silence is her only weapon.

In the lovers we see the effects of outside forces (however unusual) acting on characters in love. Though the couples eventually get married, we are left with a bit of doubt and unease. Only three characters have had the effects of the love juice reversed; one of them is still under its spell. Does that mean Demetrius's marriage is less true?

Hermia: Noel True

I think she had a very privileged upbringing and wanted for nothing. I assumed her mother died when she was very young and that she was raised solely by her father, to whom she is very close. He's her only parent and she's his only child.

Her first and only experience with love is with Lysander and everything has been wonderful thus far. She was brought up to be somebody's wife, and she doesn't understand why she can't marry the man she loves since that's what she wants. She has always gotten what she wanted, and that makes her tenacious. She is extremely surprised and aghast when she hears from her father about the "privilege of Athens," that she either marry a man she doesn't love or be put to death. I think it is the first time she's heard that the stakes were that high. (We explored in rehearsal whether her father would follow through on this and ultimately decided he wouldn't really have her put to death.) We see though that she is a strong girl, willing to stand up to her father. This resolve will get her through the challenges she faces in her later scenes.

When Lysander comes up with the plan to elope, she goes along. But she is very poorly suited to traveling through the woods. In 2.2, the scene where she and Lysander have stopped to rest and sleep and she wakes up alone, we played it different from the text. In staging, that forest was very scary and intimidating and she was initially truly terrified. In my speech, I elongated the vowels to make it sound more lonely and ominous. But that's when she rediscovers her own resolve.

This is the state she's in when she finds the other three: she has conquered her fears and she's resolved. Thus, it takes her a long time to really understand and accept what's going on. It is inconceivable to her that Lysander's feelings would have changed and that's why she hangs on so fiercely to him. The third time, Lysander finally gets through when he tells her, "I do hate thee and love Helena." Yet, she doesn't get angry at him. Instead, she turns to her best friend, the one who has been like a sister to her, and accuses her of stealing his love. In her mind, his feelings have changed because of something Helena did. Part of the comedy in this scene comes from seeing this girl of privilege turn into a scrappy kid, a fierce vixen. She may have even been a class bully. She claws and gnashes her teeth. This perfect, proper girl who had everything has been turned into a snarky, fighting machine who requires two men to hold her back. Yet her love for Lysander remains, and her last thought before falling asleep that night is still all about him: "Heaven shield Lysander if they mean a fray."

Helena: Kate Nowlin

Helena possesses a kind of high energy; she is in a hot, mad pursuit of a love. She's pining for Demetrius and has been terribly frustrated. She is totally devoted to him and doesn't really get how he could love another. It's an intellectual puzzle for her; she has kept her head and her heart separate so she considers the situation with him in logical terms. It would have been easy to play her as if she lacked self-esteem or felt deficient, but I don't think that's her. I think she's confident and sensible. Demetrius had promised his love to her but then took it back so she's trying to figure it out.

She and Hermia are best of friends, both very young with similar education and experiences. I assumed she was considered a hanger-on because of their different stations in life. Lysander doesn't really exist for her. He's like a fly. She admires the love between and Hermia and him, but that's all. She has eyes only for Demetrius and is truly devoted to him. The spaniel scene [2.1] is one of her most important scenes, and the performance of that evolved through rehearsal and the run of the production. In the beginning, I played it straight: she was very earnest in her pursuit, she didn't judge it, and there was no shame in it for her. In fact, it was a fun game. She even has her self-righteous moments when she chides him for making her woo him. Underlying it all is her true love for him.

As the run progressed, Helena also became angry. She's very intelligent and understands that she is utterly and foolishly devoted to this man who might not even be worthy. Yet, she wants him and she ultimately accepts that. She has wonderful strength and a strong conviction that her love will prevail. When she says of him in 4.1.186-87,

> *I have found Demetrius like a jewel,*
> *Mine own and not mine own.*

that was a mark of maturity and understanding. She acknowledges that she was approaching it all wrong in trying to possess him. And now he is hers, but she doesn't own him.

The lovers (Noel True as Hermia, Paris Remillard as Lysander, Kate Nowlin as Helena, and Paul Witthorne as Demetrius) learn their fate from Theseus (Mark H. Dold) as Egeus (Edward Gero) and Hippolyta (Lisa Tharps) look on
Photo: Richard Termine

Demetrius: Paul Whitthorne

Demetrius is the darker of the two lovers. While Lysander has always been in love with Hermia, he has thrown off Helena for Hermia for reasons other than love (power, politics, money). He doesn't have much passion in his speeches in the beginning, no poetry. The spaniel scene [2.1] is a turning point for him; he starts to speak with some passion. He gets frustrated when Helena doesn't accept his refusal and makes an outrageous threat with sexual connotations:

> *You do impeach your modesty too much,*
> *To leave the city and commit yourself*
> *Into the hands of one that loves you not;*
> *To trust the opportunity of night*
> *And the ill counsel of a desert place*
> *With the rich worth of your virginity.*

It was an empty threat.

Demetrius is the only one who ends the play with the love juice still on him, which is interesting. Everyone else has followed their heart, and with him, you don't really know. He is given his most poetic and romantic speech when he is recounting the events to Theseus and he makes a public declaration of his love for Helena: "I wot not by what power . . . The object and pleasure of mine eye / Is only Helena." He is at his most admirable when he is leading with his heart, and that's what the love juice does for him.

He is not the most polite to the Mechanicals during Pyramus and Thisbe, but I was playing a little bit drunk on my wedding night. I was getting chummy with the duke, showing some machismo around the other guys.

In this production, Oberon and Titania are less the imperial rulers of the fairy kingdom (though they do still rule) and instead are closer in spirit to the young lovers. Their quarrel is shown to be all too human: the result of jealousies, misunderstanding, and longing.

Oberon: Mark H. Dold

Oberon is an overgrown child who expects the world to revolve around him. When things don't go his way, everybody and everything pays the price. In 2.1, Titania has a speech describing the turmoil in nature because of their quarrel. She talks about floods, contagious fogs, drowned fields, the seasons altering, and the amazed world who "now knows not which is which." All because he doesn't get his way. I think he is jealous of the attention that Titania is paying the changeling boy and so tries to take him away from her in the guise of making the boy his page.

He is also an incurable romantic (his speeches are remarkably passionate) and he is desperately in love with Titania. Why else go to all the trouble of winning her back? The child in him has created this revenge fantasy that, unfortunately, he does have the power to follow through.

His soliloquy in 4.1 is a little window into all the things he is: he is an imperfect man, alone and in love, who feels guilty that he's manipulated his beloved and is looking for redemption. He seems so sad and truthful.

He then calls in Puck, and Oberon is king again. For him to be the king, he has to be treated like one, and Puck validates him in that role. Puck is a screw-up, yet Oberon keeps him. He is a delight for him to have around; as a master trickster, there is great pleasure to be gleaned from his activities. His toying with the lovers was silly fun, but I think Oberon also learned a bit about loving and longing. Lisa Tharps [Titania] and I were not much older than the four lovers, so I think in the casting, the play became a little bit about six madcap lovers instead of four.

Titania (Lisa Tharps) and Oberon (Mark H. Dold)
Photo: Richard Termine

Titania: Lisa Tharps

As the queen of the fairies, Titania is an extravagant force of nature. Family and camaraderie are important to her, and at her core, she just wants everything to work out. We see this in her caring for the son of a votaress and in her immediate forgiveness of Oberon's misdeed. I don't think it was a weakness that she didn't chastise him; I think she was courageous in letting go of the need for anger. She's very accepting.

The effect of the love juice on her was to enhance and exaggerate all of these qualities. Her desire of wanting to be loved and accepted was heightened and she was able to give all that to Bottom, in effect displacing her desire for Oberon. The juice also had a physical effect on her, making her feel ethereal and floaty. I was actually off the ground for most of the play, on the shoulders of an actor concealed by my voluminous skirt, so this wasn't hard.

The changeling boy is very important to me. I made a commitment to his mother and I think of him as family. Oberon wants the boy to be a soldier for him (I think he is sincere) but also because he is jealous of the child and all the attention I give him. I don't have much interaction with Puck but I think he's just a bunch of trouble, egging on Oberon.

The Mechanicals, the tradesmen who form the cast of Pyramus *and* Thisbe, *primarily provide the comedy in the play while also showing its heart. Each proclaim love and respect for each other, and their earnest and sincere efforts at performing make the point for Theseus:*

> *Love, therefore, and tongue-tied simplicity*
> *In least speak most, to my capacity.*

Quince: Edward Gero

Quince is clearly the actor-manager. He organizes everything (e.g., putting together the prop list) and he has a vision for the play. I think his company respects him. His main challenge is how to manage a star actor such as Bottom, whom he considers to be the best actor he has. There is clearly tension in their collaboration. Egeus and Quince are similar in that they are both trying to have control but find that they ultimately need to surrender it.

When Quince delivers the prologue (5.1.108-117), I was trying to figure out why he messed it up when he is perfect in his next speech. We decided that he didn't consider himself an actor so he wrote out the prologue and intended to read it. However, he accidentally drops some pages from his script and didn't realize it until it was too late and he had to speak. So his delivery was the result of him struggling to remember the lines he wrote. I played him as a deer caught in the headlights.

Robin Starveling: John Livingstone Rolle

Starveling's journey was to me about fear, the unknown, and overcoming them to rise to the occasion. The Mechanicals have gathered in their first scene to begin the process of putting together a play for the Duke's wedding day. I think that for any individual, regardless of his or her personal political views, the prospect of performing for your leader would be an honor that would hold some pride, excitement, and great trepidation.

I'm sure that the Mechanicals are well-versed in their respective trades but as thespians, they are complete novices. Nevertheless, with the direction of Peter Quince and the acting prowess of Nick Bottom, they will tackle the challenge.

For Robin Starveling to be named and thought fit among all Athenians to be with such talented men as Nick Bottom is as exciting as it is terrifying. I chose to play him as an easily excitable and sensitive man. The proposal of Peter Quince in 1.2 that they "meet in the palace wood a mile without the town" to rehearse seems a little extreme to me and downright scary. But if it means keeping our plans secret from the competition and if Nick Bottom isn't afraid to rehearse in the woods at night, then so be it.

The knowledge of the dreadful violence to be enacted in *Pyramus and Thisbe* on top of his fear of the dark woods was terribly scary and almost unbearable for Starveling. He works very hard to reduce his fear. When Bottom mentions "the ladies cannot abide Pyramus drawing a sword to kill himself," Starveling pipes up, "I believe we must leave the killing out, when all is done." And when Snout raises the question of the ladies' fear of the lion, it is then that Starveling confesses his own apprehension: "I fear it, I promise you." After Starveling witnesses Bottom's transformation he is struck dumb and there is nothing to be done but to flee. I think that when he is later sent to Bottom's house and he reports that "he [Bottom] cannot be heard of and that out of doubt he is transported," I think that it is possible that Starveling, out of fear, may not have even gone to seek out Bottom as was asked of him.

Starveling is also to "present the person" of the Moon. For me, Starveling is in all his glory and feels absolutely fabulous in his moonsuit outfit (no doubt his own handiwork). As the court looks on and rudely makes comments during the performance, Starveling's zealous desire to "shine" as the moon erupts in a diva-like momentary fit of rage that causes his partners to worry about him getting too upset to carry on. During rehearsals, we came up with the idea that Starveling should let his zealous desire to shine coupled with his being moved by Bottom's performance to allow the technical difficulty of the lantern he holds as "moonshine" to droop at various points during Pyramus death scene, much to Bottom's dismay. Towards the end, the lantern has wandered so low, shining right above Bottom's hairline as he dies, that he exasperatedly tells the enthralled and upstaging Starveling to GET OFF THE STAGE:

> *My soul is in the sky:*
> *Tongue lose thy light!*
> MOON TAKE THY FLIGHT!

For me, Starveling's journey in this play is that of a simple man over-coming his fears to realize his own potential.

Nick Bottom (David Sabin) and Robin Starveling (John Livingstone Rolle) in *Pyramus and Thisbe*
Photo: Richard Termine

Tom Snout: Ryan Artzberger

I played Tom Snout, who ends up playing The Wall in *Pyramus and Thisbe*. His main relationships in the play are with the other tradesmen, the so-called Mechanicals. His feeling about them in general is (to borrow from *Henry V*) of a band of brothers. Specifically, for Quince he feels a quiet respect and a lit-tle resentment that he gets to be the director. Bottom is the greatest actor Snout can imagine, and as a result, Snout has for Bottom the deepest imaginable admiration spilling over into awe. He also feels fortunate that he gets to call him his colleague and friend though it's doubtful Bottom feels that way about him. The scene that's most important to him would seem to be the play within the play, but I think the scene in which Bottom returns is the scene that contains the event that's most important to Snout—the restoration of Bottom after his horrible transformation and the return of his idol. After that, performing with him in front of royalty is just icing on the cake.

Francis Flute: Greg Felden

Francis Flute is a shy young man who feels he has great untapped potential. He is very excited to be a part of the play and may even have an artistic temperament, but in the beginning doesn't quite know his place. For me, he is that guy who is awkwardly carrying a great deal of intelligence and emotion, and is therefore the butt of the teasing from the rough Mechanicals, but I believe he is destined to blossom.

The Mechanicals: Francis Flute (Greg Felden), Robin Starveling (John Livingstone Rolle), Nick Bottom (David Sabin) , Tom Snout (Ryan Artzberger), Peter Quince (Edward Gero), and Snug (Brad Waller)
Photo: Richard Termine

Flute reveres Bottom. He admires his courage and virtuosity, and secretly longs to be like him one day. He is a bit frightened of the controlling and impatient Quince, and struggles to fit in with "the guys." The apparent loss of Bottom that precedes the play within the play is a very emotional experience for Flute. He seems more worried about him than the others—he speaks more in that scene than any other so far, yet after Bottom returns, he is silent. I believe he is overwhelmed. During their performance for the court, when Flute watches Bottom portray his death, Flute's emotions surrounding Bottom's disappearance are awakened. They then fuel Flute's own death speech. He is transported and actually achieves a great bit of acting.

Unfortunately, David Sabin, who played Bottom, was unavailable for interview. Mark Lamos, the director, steps in to talk about David, his portrayal of Bottom, and the Mechanicals.

Director: Mark Lamos

The group of actors who played the Mechanicals had all worked together in the past. Their comfort with each other, their bonhomie, really informed the production. David's Bottom was wildly egotistical but not too brash or pushy. He was driven by his love of the theatre, and his exuberance was contagious. There was a sweetness about him [that many reviewers of the production noted] that made people adore every moment he was on stage. The initial thought about his character was to be more "Actor-like," an over-the-top John Barrymore, and the original costume for Bottom fit that idea. When I saw what David was like and what he brought to the role, he and I chatted with the costume designer and she revised everything.

We wanted the whole love scene with Titania to not be necessarily funny but to be loving. David is older than the usual Bottom and he was so warm and dear that the scene was terribly touching. When he was interacting with the fairies beforehand, it was a very positive feeling, as if he were reinvigorating or blessing them. His being with Titania was an exalted thing, which we stressed by having the chaise lounge on which they were laying be lifted up above, as if to the heavens. Bottom is a changed man after that. He gains in depth, as do the Mechanicals. Even Oberon is ennobled. It is after he sees them that feels remorse and pity, orders Puck to set things right, and releases Titania from the spell.

Finally, the creature responsible for the aforementioned ass's head and for much of the mischief in the play: Puck. He is portrayed as a gleeful child, not meaning to be malicious and just enjoying himself.

Daniel Breaker as Puck
Photo: Richard Termine

Puck: Daniel Breaker

Puck is just a little child who enjoys causing mischief. I play him with all the wide-eyed innocence and humor of a two-year-old. Oberon is his best friend, father figure, and big brother all in one. Puck jokes with him, makes him smile, and exasperates him. Oberon needs me in order to feel like a king.

He really doesn't have much of a relationship with others in the play. He talks to a fairy and cast spells on the lovers, and that's all. He has an amazing bag of tricks: he can cast spells, throw his voice, lead people around. He is so completely playful, joyous, and innocent, yet his actions have great consequences. Oberon watches out for him and makes him set things right.

We officially end the play right before Puck's last speech. As soon as Titania and Oberon say their last lines, the magic of the play starts to fade. Puck
takes his hat off, and I address the audience as myself. I deliver the final
speech as Daniel Breaker. Then all of the actors come out, also as themselves,
to take their bows.

A Voice Coach's Perspective on Speaking Shakespeare

KEEPING SHAKESPEARE PRACTICAL

Andrew Wade

track 47-48

Introduction to Speaking Shakespeare: Derek Jacobi
Speaking Shakespeare: Andrew Wade with Drew Cortese

Why, you might be wondering, is it so important to keep Shakespeare practical? What do I mean by practical? Why is this the way to discover how to speak the text and understand it?

Plays themselves are not simply literary events—they demand interpreters in the deepest sense of the word, and the language of Shakespeare requires, therefore, not a vocal demonstration of writing techniques but an imaginative response to that writing. The key word here is imagination. The task of the voice coach is to offer relevant choices to the actor so that the actor's imagination is titillated, excited by the language, which he or she can then share with an audience, playing on that audience's imagination. Take the word "IF"—it is only composed of two letters when written, but if you say it aloud and listen to what it implies, then your reaction, the way the word plays through you, can change the perception of meaning. "Iffffffff"… you might hear and feel it implying "possibilities," "choices," "questioning," "trying to work something out." The saying of this word provokes active investigation of thought. What an apt word to launch a play: "If music be the food of love, play on" (Act 1, Scene 1 in *Twelfth Night, or What You Will*). How this word engages the listener and immediately sets up an involvement is about more than audibility. How we verbalize sounds has a direct link to meaning and understanding. In the words of Touchstone in *As You Like It*, "Much virtue in if."

I was working with a company in Vancouver on *Macbeth,* and at the end of the first week's rehearsal—after having explored our voices and opening out different pieces of text to hear the possibilities of the rhythm, feeling how the meter affects the thinking and feeling, looking at structure and form— one of the actors admitted he was also a writer of soap operas and that I had completely changed his way of writing. Specifically, in saying a line like, "The multitudinous seas incarnadine / Making the green one red" he heard the complexity of meaning revealed in the use of polysyllabic words becoming monosyllabic, layered upon the words' individual dictionary definitions. The writer was reminded that merely reproducing the speech of everyday life was nowhere near as powerful and effective as language that is shaped.

Do you think soap operas would benefit from rhyming couplets? Somehow this is difficult to imagine! But, the writer's comments set me thinking. As I am constantly trying to find ways of exploring the acting process, of opening out actors' connection with language that isn't their own, I thought it would be a good idea to involve writers and actors in some practical work on language. After talking to Cicely Berry (Voice Director, the Royal Shakespeare Company) and Colin Chambers (the then RSC Production Adviser), we put together a group of writers and actors who were interested in taking part. It was a fascinating experience all round, and it broke down barriers and misconceptions.

The actors discovered, for instance, that a writer is not coming from a very different place as they are in their creative search; that an idea or an image may result from a struggle to define a gut feeling and not from some crafted, well-formed idea in the head. The physical connection of language to the body was reaffirmed. After working with a group on Yeats' poem *Easter 1916*, Ann Devlin changed the title of the play she was writing for the Royal Shakespeare Company to *After Easter*. She had experienced the poem read aloud by a circle of participants, each voice becoming a realization of the shape of the writing. Thus it made a much fuller impact on her and caused her thinking to shift. Such practical exchanges, through language work and voice, feed and stimulate my work to go beyond making sure the actors' voices are technically sound.

It is, of course, no different when we work on a Shakespeare play. A similar connection with the language is crucial. Playing Shakespeare, in many ways, is crafted instinct. The task is thus to find the best way to tap into someone's imagination. As Peter Brook put it: "People forget that a text is dumb. To make it speak, one must create a communication machine. A living network, like a nervous system, must be made if a text which comes from far away is to touch the sensibility of the present."

This journey is never to be taken for granted. It is the process that every text must undergo every time it is staged. There is no definitive rehearsal that would solve problems or indicate ways of staging a given play. Again, this is where creative, practical work on voice can help forge new meaning by offering areas of exploration and challenge. The central idea behind my work comes back to posing the question, "How does meaning change by speaking out aloud?" It would be unwise to jump hastily to the end process for, as Peter Brook says, "Shakespeare's words are records of the words that he wanted spoken, words issuing from people's mouths, with pitch, pause and rhythm and gesture as part of their meaning. A word does not start as a word—it is the end product which begins as an impulse, stimulated by attitude and behavior which dictates the need for expression." (1)

PRACTICALLY SPEAKING

Something happens when we vocalize, when we isolate sounds, when we start to speak words aloud, when we put them to the test of our physicality, of our anatomy. We expose ourselves in a way that makes taking the language back more difficult. Our body begins a debate with itself, becomes alive with the vibrations of sound produced in the mouth or rooted deep in the muscles that aim at defining sound. In fact, the spoken words bring into play all the senses, before sense and another level of meaning are reached.

"How do I know what I think, until I see what I say," Oscar Wilde once said. A concrete illustration of this phrase was reported to me when I was leading a workshop recently. A grandmother said the work we had done that day reminded her of what her six-year-old grandson had said to his mother while they were driving through Wales: "Look, mummy, sheep! Sheep! Sheep!" "You don't have to keep telling us," the mother replied, but the boy said, "How do I know they're there, if I don't tell you?!"

Therefore, when we speak of ideas, of sense, we slightly take for granted those physical processes which affect and change their meaning. We tend to separate something that is an organic whole. In doing so, we become blind to the fact that it is precisely this physical connection to the words that enables the actors to make the language theirs.

The struggle for meaning is not just impressionistic theater mystique; it is an indispensable aspect of the rehearsal process and carries on during the life of every production. In this struggle, practical work on Shakespeare is vital and may help spark creativity and shed some light on the way meaning is born into language. After a performance of *More Words*, a show devised and directed by Cicely Berry and myself, Katie Mitchell (a former artistic director of The Other Place in Stratford-upon-Avon) gave me an essay by Ted Hughes that echoes with the piece. In it, Ted Hughes compares the writing of a poem—the coming into existence of words—to the capture of a wild animal. You will notice that in the following passage Hughes talks of "spirit" or "living parts" but never of "thought" or "sense." With great care and precaution, he advises, "It is better to call [the poem] an assembly of living parts moved by a single spirit. The living parts are the words, the images, the rhythms. The spirit is the life which inhabits them when they all work together. It is impossible to say which comes first, parts or spirit."

This is also true of life in words, as many are connected directly to one or several of our senses. Here Hughes talks revealingly of "the five senses," of "word," "action," and "muscle," all things which a practical approach to language is more likely to allow one to perceive and do justice to.

Words that live are those which we hear, like "click" or "chuckle," or which we see, like "freckled" or "veined," or which we taste, like "vinegar" or "sugar," or touch, like "prickle" or "oily," or smell, like "tar" or "onion," words which belong to one of the five senses. Or words that act and seem to use their muscles, like "flick" or "balance." (2)

In this way, practically working on Shakespeare to arrive at understanding lends itself rather well, I think, to what Adrian Noble (former artistic director of the RSC) calls "a theater of poetry," a form of art that, rooted deeply in its classical origins, would seek to awaken the imagination of its audiences through love and respect for words while satisfying our eternal craving for myths and twice-told tales.

This can only be achieved at some cost. There is indeed a difficult battle to fight and hopefully win "the battle of the word to survive." This phrase was coined by Michael Redgrave at the beginning of the 1950s, a period when theater began to be deeply influenced by more physical forms, such as mime. (3) Although the context is obviously different, the fight today is of the same nature.

LISTENING TO SHAKESPEARE

Because of the influence of television, our way of speaking as well as listening has changed. It is crucial to be aware of this. We can get fairly close to the way *Henry V* or *Hamlet* was staged in Shakespeare's time; we can try also to reconstruct the way English was spoken. But somehow, all these fall short of the real and most important goal: the Elizabethan ear. How did one "hear" a Shakespeare play? This is hardest to know. My personal view is that we will probably never know for sure. We are, even when we hear a Shakespeare play or a recording from the past, bound irrevocably to modernity. The Elizabethan ear was no doubt different from our own, as people were not spoken to or entertained in the same way. A modern voice has to engage us in a different way in order to make us truly listen in a society that seems to rely solely on the belief that image is truth, that it is more important to show than to tell.

Sometimes, we say that a speech in Shakespeare, or even an entire production, is not well-spoken, not up to standard. What do we mean by that? Evidently, there are a certain number of "guidelines" that any actor now has to know when working on a classical text. Yet, even when these are known, actors still have to make choices when they speak. A sound is not a sound without somebody to lend an ear to it: rhetoric is nothing without an audience.

There are a certain number of factors that affect the receiver's ear. These can be cultural factors such as the transition between different acting styles or the level of training that our contemporary ear has had. There are also personal and emotional factors. Often we feel the performance was not well-spoken because, somehow, it did not live up to our expectations of how we think it should have been performed. Is it that many of us have a self-conscious model, perhaps our own first experience of Shakespeare, that meant something to us and became our reference point for the future (some treasured performance kept under glass)? Nothing from then on can quite compare with that experience.

Most of the time, however, it is more complex than nostalgia. Take, for example, the thorny area of accent. I remind myself constantly that audibility is not embedded in Received Pronunciation or Standard American. The familiarity that those in power have with speech and the articulate confidence gained from coming from the right quarters can lead us all to hear certain types of voices as outshining others. But, to my mind, the role of theater is at least to question these assumptions so that we do not perpetuate those givens but work towards a broader tolerance.

In Canada on a production of *Twelfth Night*, I was working with an actor who was from Newfoundland. His own natural rhythms in speaking seemed completely at home with Shakespeare's. Is this because his root voice has direct links back to the voice of Shakespeare's time? It does seem that compared to British dialects, which are predominantly about pitch, many North American dialects have a wonderful respect and vibrancy in their use of vowels. Shakespeare's language seems to me very vowel-aware. How useful it is for an actor to isolate the vowels in the spoken words to hear the music they produce, the rich patterns, their direct connection to feelings. North Americans more easily respond to this and allow it to feed their speaking. I can only assume it is closer to how the Elizabethans spoke.

In *Othello* the very names of the characters have a direct connection to one vowel in particular. All the male names, except the Duke, end in the sound OH: Othello, Cassio, Iago, Brabantio, etc. Furthermore, the sound OH ripples through the play both consciously and unconsciously. "Oh" occurs repeatedly and, more interestingly, is contained within other words: "so," "soul," and "know." These words resonate throughout the play, reinforcing another level of meaning. The repeating of the same sounds affects us beyond what we can quite say.

Vowels come from deep within us, from our very core. We speak vowels before we speak consonants. They seem to reveal the feelings that require the consonants to give the shape to what we perceive as making sense.

Working with actors who are bilingual (or ones for whom English is not the native language) is fascinating because of the way it allows the actor to have an awareness of the cadence in Shakespeare. There seems to be an objective perception to the musical patterns in the text, and the use of alliteration and assonance are often more easily heard not just as literary devices, but also as means by which meaning is formed and revealed to an audience.

Every speech pattern (i.e., accent, rhythm) is capable of audibility. Each has its own music, each can become an accent when juxtaposed against another. The point at which a speech pattern becomes audible is in the dynamic of the physical making of those sounds. The speaker must have the desire to get through to a listener and must be confident that every speech pattern has a right to be heard.

SPEAKING SHAKESPEARE

So, the way to speak Shakespeare is not intrinsically tied to a particular sound; rather, it is how a speaker energetically connects to that language. Central to this is how we relate to the form of Shakespeare. Shakespeare employs verse, prose, and rhetorical devices to communicate meaning. For example, in *Romeo and Juliet*, the use of contrasts helps us to quantify Juliet's feelings: "And learn me how to lose a winning match," "Whiter than new snow upon a raven's back." These extreme opposites, "lose" and "winning," "new snow" and "raven's back," are her means to express and make sense of her feelings.

On a more personal note, I am often reminded how much, as an individual, I owe to Shakespeare's spoken word. The rather quiet and inarticulate schoolboy I once was found in the speaking and the acting of those words a means to quench his thirst for expression.

NOTES:
(1) Peter Brook, *The Empty Space* (Harmondsworth: Penguin, 1972)
(2) Ted Hughes, *Winter Pollen* (London: Faber and Faber, 1995)
(3) Michael Redgrave, *The Actor's Ways and Means*
     (London: Heinemann, 1951)

In the Age of Shakespeare

Thomas Garvey

One of the earliest published pictures of Shakespeare's birthplace, from an original watercolor by Phoebe Dighton (1834)

The works of William Shakespeare have won the love of millions since he first set pen to paper some four hundred years ago, but at first blush, his plays can seem difficult to understand, even willfully obscure. There are so many strange words: not fancy, exactly, but often only half-familiar. And the very fabric of the language seems to spring from a world of forgotten assumptions, a vast network of beliefs and superstitions that have long been dispelled from the modern mind.

In fact, when "Gulielmus filius Johannes Shakespeare" (Latin for "William, son of John Shakespeare") was baptized in Stratford-on-Avon in 1564, English itself was only just settling into its current form; no dictionary had yet been written, and Shakespeare coined hundreds of words himself. Astronomy and medicine were entangled with astrology and the occult arts; democracy was waiting to be reborn; and even educated people believed in witches and fairies, and that the sun revolved around the Earth. Yet somehow Shakespeare still speaks to us today, in a voice as fresh and direct as the day his lines were first spoken, and to better understand both their artistic depth and enduring power, we must first understand something of his age.

REVOLUTION AND RELIGION

Shakespeare was born into a nation on the verge of global power, yet torn by religious strife. Henry VIII, the much-married father of Elizabeth I, had

From *The Book of Martyrs* (1563), this woodcut shows the Archbishop of Canterbury being burned at the stake in March 1556

Map of London ca. 1625

defied the Pope by proclaiming a new national church, with himself as its head. After Henry's death, however, his daughter Mary reinstituted Catholicism via a murderous nationwide campaign, going so far as to burn the Archbishop of Canterbury at the stake. But after a mere five years, the childless Mary also died, and when her half-sister Elizabeth was crowned, she declared the Church of England again triumphant.

In the wake of so many religious reversals, it is impossible to know which form of faith lay closest to the English heart, and at first, Elizabeth was content with mere outward deference to the Anglican Church. Once the Pope hinted her assassination would not be a mortal sin, however, the suppression of Catholicism grew more savage, and many Catholics—including some known in Stratford—were hunted down and executed, which meant being hanged, disemboweled, and carved into quarters. Many scholars suspect that Shakespeare himself was raised a Catholic (his father's testament of faith was found hidden in his childhood home). We can speculate about the impact this religious tumult may have had on his plays. Indeed, while explicit Catholic themes, such as the description of Purgatory in *Hamlet*, are rare, the larger themes of disguise and double allegiance are prominent across the canon. Prince Hal offers false friendship to Falstaff in the histories, the heroines of the comedies are forced to disguise themselves as men, and the action of the tragedies is driven by double-dealing villains. "I am not what I am," Iago tells us (and himself) in *Othello*, summing up in a single stroke what may have been Shakespeare's formative social and spiritual experience.

If religious conflict rippled beneath the body politic like some ominous undertow, on its surface the tide of English power was clearly on the rise. The defeat of the Spanish Armada in 1588 had established Britain as a global power; by 1595 Sir Walter Raleigh had founded the colony of Virginia (named for the Virgin Queen), and discovered a new crop, tobacco, which would inspire a burgeoning international trade. After decades of strife and the threat of invasion, England enjoyed a welcome stability. As the national coffers grew, so did London; over the course of Elizabeth's reign, the city would nearly double in size to a population of some 200,000.

Hornbook from Shakespeare's lifetime

A 1639 engraving of a scene from a royal state visit of Marie de Medici depicts London's packed, closely crowded half-timbered houses.

FROM COUNTRY TO COURT

The urban boom brought a new dimension to British life—the mentality of the metropolis. By contrast, in Stratford-on-Avon, the rhythms of the rural world still held sway. Educated in the local grammar school, Shakespeare was taught to read and write by a schoolmaster called an "abecedarian", and as he grew older, he was introduced to logic, rhetoric, and Latin. Like most schoolboys of his time, he was familiar with Roman mythology and may have learned a little Greek, perhaps by translating passages of the New Testament. Thus while he never attended a university, Shakespeare could confidently refer in his plays to myths and legends that today we associate with the highly educated.

Beyond the classroom, however, he was immersed in the life of the countryside, and his writing all but revels in its flora and fauna, from the wounded deer of *As You Like It* to the herbs and flowers which Ophelia scatters in *Hamlet*. Pagan rituals abounded in the rural villages of Shakespeare's day, where residents danced around maypoles in spring, performed "mummers' plays" in winter, and recited rhymes year-round to ward off witches and fairies.

The custom most pertinent to Shakespeare's art was the medieval "mystery play," in which moral allegories were enacted in country homes and village squares by troupes of traveling actors. These strolling players—usually four men and two boys who played the women's roles—often lightened the moralizing with bawdy interludes in a mix of high and low feeling, which would become a defining feature of Shakespeare's art. Occasionally even a professional troupe, such as Lord Strange's Men, or the Queen's Men, would arrive in town, perhaps coming straight to Shakespeare's door (his father was the town's bailiff) for permission to perform.

Rarely, however, did such troupes stray far from their base in London, the nation's rapidly expanding capital and cultural center. The city itself had existed since the time of the Romans (who built the original London Bridge), but it was not until the Renaissance that its population spilled beyond its ancient walls and began to grow along (and across) the Thames, by whose banks the Tudors had built their glorious palaces. It was these two contradictory worlds—a modern metropolis cheek-by-jowl with a medieval court—that provided the two very different audiences who applauded Shakespeare's plays.

Londoners both high and low craved distraction. Elizabeth's court constantly celebrated her reign with dazzling pageants and performances that required a local pool of professional actors and musicians. Beyond the graceful landscape of the royal parks, however, the general populace was packed into little more than a square mile of cramped and crooked streets where theatrical entertainment was frowned upon as compromising public morals.

Just outside the jurisdiction of the city fathers, however, across the twenty arches of London Bridge on the south bank of the Thames, lay the wilder district of "Southwark." A grim reminder of royal power lay at the end of the bridge—the decapitated heads of traitors stared down from pikes at passersby. Once beyond their baleful gaze, people found the amusements they desired, and their growing numbers meant a market suddenly existed for daily entertainment. Bear-baiting and cockfighting flourished, along with taverns, brothels, and even the new institution of the theater.

Southwark, as depicted in Hollar's long view of London (1647). Blackfriars is on the top right and the labels of Bear-baiting and the Globe were inadvertently reversed.

THE ADVENT OF THE THEATRE

The first building in England designed for the performance of plays—called, straightforwardly enough, "The Theatre"—was built in London when Shakespeare was still a boy. It was owned by James Burbage, father of Richard Burbage, who would become Shakespeare's lead actor in the acting company The Lord Chamberlain's Men. "The Theatre," consciously or unconsciously, resembled the yards in which traveling players had long plied their trade—it was an open-air polygon, with three tiers of galleries surrounding a canopied stage in a flat central yard, which was ideal for the athletic competitions the building also hosted. The innovative arena must have found an appreciative audience, for it was soon joined by the Curtain, and then the Rose, which was the first theater to rise in Southwark among the brothels, bars, and bear-baiting pits.

Even as these new venues were being built, a revolution in the drama itself was taking place. Just as Renaissance artists turned to classical models for inspiration, so English writers looked to Roman verse as a prototype for the new national drama. "Blank verse," or iambic pentameter (that is, a poetic line with five alternating stressed and unstressed syllables), was an adaptation of Latin forms, and first appeared in England in a translation of Virgil's *Aeneid*. Blank verse was first spoken on stage in 1561, in the now-forgotten *Gorboduc*, but it was not until the brilliant Christopher Marlowe (born the same year as Shakespeare) transformed it into the "mighty line" of such plays as *Tamburlaine* (1587) that the power and flexibility of the form made it the baseline of English drama.

Marlowe—who, unlike Shakespeare, had attended college—led the "university wits," a clique of hard-living free thinkers who in between all manner of exploits managed to define a new form of theater. The dates of Shakespeare's arrival in London are unknown—we have no record of him in Stratford after 1585—but by the early 1590s he had already absorbed the essence of Marlowe's invention, and begun producing astonishing innovations of his own.

While the "university wits" had worked with myth and fantasy, however, Shakespeare turned to a grand new theme, English history—penning the three-part saga of *Henry VI* in or around 1590. The trilogy was such a success that Shakespeare became the envy of his circle—one unhappy competitor, Robert Greene, even complained in 1592 of "an upstart crow...beautified with our feathers...[who is] in his own conceit the only Shake-scene in a country."

Such jibes perhaps only confirmed Shakespeare's estimation of himself, for he began to apply his mastery of blank verse in all directions, succeeding at tragedy (*Titus Andronicus*), farce (*The Comedy of Errors*), and romantic comedy (*The Two Gentlemen of Verona*). He drew his plots from everywhere: existing poems, romances, folk tales, even other plays. In fact a number of Shakespeare's dramas (*Hamlet* included) may be revisions of earlier texts owned by his troupe. Since copyright laws did not exist, acting companies usually kept their texts close to their chests, only allowing publication when a play was no longer popular, or, conversely, when a play was *so* popular (as with *Romeo and Juliet*) that unauthorized versions had already been printed.

Demand for new plays and performance venues steadily increased. Soon, new theaters (the Hope and the Swan) joined the Rose in Southwark, followed shortly by the legendary Globe, which opened in 1600. (After some trouble with their lease, Shakespeare's acting troupe, the Lord

pendeſt on ſo meane a ſtay . Baſe minded men all three of you, if by my miſerie you be not warnd:for vnto none of you (like mee) ſought thoſe burres to cleaue : thoſe Puppets (I meane) that ſpake from our mouths, thoſe Anticks garniſht in our colours. Is it not ſtrange, that I, to whom they all haue beene beholding: is it not like that you, to whome they all haue beene beholding, ſhall (were yee in that caſe as I am now) bee both at once of them forſaken? Yes truſt them not : for there is an vp-ſtart Crow, beautified with our feathers, that with his Tygers hart wrapt in a Players hyde, ſuppoſes he is as well able to bombaſt out a blanke verſe as the beſt of you : and beeing an abſolute Iohannes fac totum, is in his owne conceit the onely Shake-ſcene in a countrey. O that I might intreat your rare wits to be imploied in more profitable courſes : & let thoſe Apes imitate your paſt excellence, and neuer more acquaint them with your admired inuentions . I knowe the beſt huſband of

Greene's insult, lines 9–14

Chamberlain's Men, had disassembled "The Theatre" and transported its timbers across the Thames, using them as the structure for the Globe.) Shakespeare was a shareholder in this new venture, with its motto "All the world's a stage," and continued to write and perform for it as well. Full-length plays were now being presented every afternoon but Sunday, and the public appetite for new material seemed endless.

The only curb on the public's hunger for theater was its fear of the plague—for popular belief held the disease was easily spread in crowds. Even worse, the infection was completely beyond the powers of Elizabethan medicine, which held that health derived from four "humors" or internal fluids identified as bile, phlegm, blood, and choler. Such articles of faith, however, were utterly ineffective against a genuine health crisis, and in times of plague, the authorities' panicked response was to shut down any venue where large crowds might congregate. The theaters would be closed for lengthy periods in 1593, 1597, and 1603, during which times Shakespeare was forced to play at court, tour the provinces, or, as many scholars believe, write what would become his famous cycle of sonnets.

THE NEXT STAGE

Between these catastrophic closings, the theater thrived as the great medium of its day; it functioned as film, television, and radio combined as well as a venue for music and dance (all performances, even tragedies, ended with a dance). Moreover, the theater was the place to see and be seen; for a penny

Famous scale model of the Globe completed by Dr. John Cranford Adams in 1954. Collectively, 25,000 pieces were used in constructing the replica. Dr. Adams used walnut to imitate the timber of the Globe, plaster was placed with a spoon and medicine dropper, and 6,500 tiny "bricks" measured by pencil eraser strips were individually placed on the model.

you could stand through a performance in the yard, a penny more bought you a seat in the galleries, while yet another purchased you a cushion. The wealthy, the poor, the royal, and the common all gathered at the Globe, and Shakespeare designed his plays—with their action, humor, and highly refined poetry—not only to satisfy their divergent tastes but also to respond to their differing points of view. In the crucible of Elizabethan theater, the various classes could briefly see themselves as others saw them, and drama could genuinely show "the age and body of the time his form and pressure," to quote Hamlet himself.

In order to accommodate his expanding art, the simplicity of the Elizabethan stage had developed a startling flexibility. The canopied platform of the Globe had a trap in its floor for sudden disappearances, while an alcove at the rear, between the pillars supporting its roof, allowed for "discoveries" and interior space. Above, a balcony made possible the love scene in *Romeo and Juliet*; while still higher, the thatched roof could double as a tower or rampart. And though the stage was largely free of scenery, the costumes were sumptuous—a theater troupe's clothing was its greatest asset. Patrons were used to real drums banging in battle scenes and real cannons firing overhead (in fact, a misfire would one day set the Globe aflame).

With the death of Elizabeth, and the accession of James I to the throne in 1603, Shakespeare only saw his power and influence grow. James, who considered himself an intellectual and something of a scholar, took over the patronage of the Lord Chamberlain's Men, renaming them the King's Men; the troupe even marched in his celebratory entrance to London. At this pinnacle of both artistic power and prestige, Shakespeare composed *Othello*, *King Lear*, and *Macbeth* in quick succession, and soon the King's Men acquired a new, indoor theater in London, which allowed the integration of more music and spectacle into his work. At this wildly popular venue, Shakespeare developed a new form of drama that scholars have dubbed "the romance," which combined elements of comedy and tragedy in a magnificent vision that would culminate in the playwright's last masterpiece, *The Tempest*. Not long after this final innovation, Shakespeare retired to Stratford a wealthy and prominent gentleman.

BEYOND THE ELIZABETHAN UNIVERSE

This is how Shakespeare fit into his age. But how did he transcend it? The answer lies in the plays themselves. For even as we see in the surface of his drama the belief system of England in the sixteenth century, Shakespeare himself is always questioning his own culture, holding its ideas up to the light and shaking them, sometimes hard. In the case of the Elizabethan faith in astrology, Shakespeare had his villain Edmund sneer, "We make guilty of our disasters the sun, the moon, and stars; as if we were villains on necessity." When pondering the medieval code of chivalry, Falstaff decides, "The better part of valor is discretion." The divine right of kings is questioned in *Richard II*, and the inferior status of women—a belief that survived even the crowning of Elizabeth—appears ridiculous before the brilliant examples of Portia (*The Merchant of Venice*), and Rosalind (*As You Like It*). Perhaps it is through this constant shifting of perspective, this relentless sense of exploration, that the playwright somehow outlived the limits of his own period, and became, in the words of his rival Ben Jonson, "not just for an age, but for all time."

track 49

Conclusion of the Sourcebooks Shakespeare
A Midsummer Night's Dream: *Derek Jacobi*

About the Online Teaching Resources

The Sourcebooks Shakespeare is committed to supporting students and educators in the study of Shakespeare. A website with additional articles and essays, extended audio, a forum for discussions, and other resources can be found (starting in August 2006) at www.sourcebooksshakespeare.com. To illustrate how the Sourcebooks Shakespeare may be used in your class, Jeremy Ehrlich, the head of education at the Folger Shakespeare Library, contributed an essay called "Working with Audio in the Classroom." The following is an excerpt:

One possible way of approaching basic audio work in the classroom is shown in the handout [on the site]. It is meant to give some guidance for the first-time user of audio in the classroom. I would urge you to adapt this to the particular circumstances and interests of your own students.

To use it, divide the students into four groups. Assign each group one of the four technical elements of audio—volume, pitch, pace, and pause—to follow as you play them an audio clip or clips. In the first section, have them record what they hear: the range they encounter in the clip and the places where their element changes. In the second section, have them suggest words for the tone of the passage based in part on their answers to the first. Sections three and four deal with tools of the actor. Modern acting theory finds the actor's objective is his single most important acting choice; an actor may then choose from a variety of tactics in order to achieve that objective. Thus, if a character's objective on stage is to get sympathy from his scene partner, he may start out by complaining, then shift to another tactic (asking for sympathy directly? throwing a tantrum?) if the first tactic fails. Asking your students to try to explain what they think a character is trying to get, and how she is trying to do it, is a way for them to follow this process through closely. Finally, the handout asks students to think about the meaning (theme) of the passage, concluding with a traditional and important tool of text analysis.

As you can see, this activity is more interesting and, probably, easier for students when it's used with multiple versions of the same piece of text. While defining an actor's motivation is difficult in a vacuum, doing so in relation to another performance may be easier: one Othello may be more concerned with gaining respect, while another Othello may be more concerned with obtaining love, for instance. This activity may be done outside of a group setting, although for students doing this work for the first time I suggest group work so they will be able to share answers on some potentially thought-provoking questions . . .

For the complete essay, please visit www.sourcebooksshakespeare.com.

Acknowledgments

The series editors wish to give heartfelt thanks to the advisory editors on *A Midsummer Night's Dream*, David Bevington and Peter Holland, whose brilliance, keen judgment, and timely advice were irreplaceable during the process of assembling this book.

We are incredibly grateful to the community of Shakespeare scholars for their generosity in sharing their talents, collections, and even their address books. We would not have been able to together such an august list of contributors without their help. First, a sincere thanks to our text editor, Terri A. Bourus, not just for her impeccable work, but also sharing her passion with us. Thanks as well to Tom Garvey, Doug Lanier, Peter Holland, and Andrew Wade for their marvelous essays, and to Jeremy Ehrlich for his fabulous essay contribution to our website. Extra appreciation goes to Doug Lanier for all his guidance and the use of his personal Shakespeare collection and to Peter Holland for pulling double duty with his essay. We want to acknowledge the editors of our other editions who have contributed much to the series: Rob Ormsby, and William Williams. We are grateful to William for his continuing guidance on textual issues, though any errors in this edition are ours.

We want to single out Tanya Gough, the proprietor of The Poor Yorick Shakespeare Catalog, for all her efforts on behalf of the series. She was an early supporter, providing encouragement from the very beginning and jumping in with whatever we needed. For her encyclopedic knowledge of Shakespeare on film and audio, for sharing her experience and collaborating on the narration script, for introducing us into her estimable network, and for a myriad of other contributions too numerous to mention, we offer our deepest gratitude.

Our research was aided immensely by the wonderful staff at Shakespeare archives and libraries around the world: Jane Edmonds and Ellen Charendoff from the Stratford Festival Archives; David Way, Richard Fairman, and the Sound Archives group from the British Library; Susan Brock and the staff at The Shakespeare Birthplace Trust; Georgianna Ziegler, Richard Kuhta, Jeremy Erlich, and everyone at the Folger Shakespeare Library; Lynne Farrington from the Annenberg Rare Book & Manuscript Library at the University of Pennsylvania; and Gene Rinkel, Bruce Swann, Nuala

Koetter, and Madeline Gibson, from the Rare Books and Special Collections Library at the University of Illinois. These individuals were instrumental in helping us gather audio: Carly Wilford, Justyn Baker, Janet Benson, and Linn Lancett-Miles. We appreciated all your help.

From the world of drama, the following shared their passion with us and helped us develop the series into a true partnership between between the artistic and academic communities. We are indebted to: Liza Holtmeier, Lauren Beyea, Catherine Weidner, and the team from The Shakespeare Theatre Company, Drew Cortese, Joe Plummer, Marilyn Halperin and the team at Chicago Shakespeare Theater, Amy Richard and the team at the Oregon Shakespeare Festival, George Joseph, Michal Daniel, Richard Termine, the 2004 cast from The Shakespeare Theatre Company in Washington, DC, and Nancy Becker of The Shakespeare Society.

With respect to the audio, we extend our heartfelt thanks to our narrating team: our director, John Tydeman, our esteemed narrator, Sir Derek Jacobi, and the staff of Motivation Studios. John has been a wonderful, generous resource to us and we look forward to future collaborations. We owe a debt of gratitude to Nicolas Soames for introducing us and for being unfailingly helpful. Thanks also to the "Speaking Shakespeare" team: Andrew Wade, Drew Cortese, and Lyron Bennett for that wonderful recording.

Our personal thanks for their kindness and unstinting support go to our friends and our extended families.

Finally, thanks to everyone at Sourcebooks who contributed their talents in realizing The Sourcebooks Shakespeare—in particular, Samantha Raue, Todd Stocke, Megan Dempster, and Katie Fetter.

Audio Credits

In all cases, we have attempted to provide archival audio in its original form. While we have tried to achieve the best possible quality on the archival audio, some audio quality is the result of source limitations.

Archival audio research by Marie Macaisa.

Narration script by Tanya Gough and Marie Macaisa.

Audio editing by Motivation Sound Studios, Marie Macaisa, and Todd Stocke.

Narration recording, audio engineering, and mastering by Motivation Sound Studios, London, UK.

Recording for "Speaking Shakespeare" by Sotti Records, New York City, USA.

The following are under license from Naxos of America www.naxousa.com ℗ HNH International Ltd. All rights reserved.
Tracks 4, 7, 10, 13, 15, 16, 19, 22, 25, 27, 28, 31, 33, 34, 37, 40

The following are selection from The Complete Arkangel Shakespeare ℗ 2003, with permission of The Audio Partners Publishing Corporation. All rights reserved. Unabridged audio dramatizations of all 38 plays. For more information, visit www.audiopartners.com/shakespeare
Tracks 3, 6, 9, 12, 18, 21, 24, 30, 36, 39, 42, 45

The following are under license from IPC Media. All rights reserved.
Tracks 43, 46

"Speaking Shakespeare" (Track 48) courtesy of Andrew Wade and Drew Cortese.

Photo Credits

Every effort has been made to correctly attribute all the materials reproduced in this book. If any errors have been made, we will be happy to correct them in future editions.

Photos and images from the March 23, 1954 staging at the Shakespeare Memorial Theatre and from the 1948 staging at the Old Vic, both directed by George Devine, are courtesy of the Rare Book and Special Collections Library, University of Illinois at Urbana-Champaign. Photos are credited on the pages on which they appear.

Photos from the Shakespeare Theatre Company's 2003–04 production directed by Mark Lamos are copyright © 2005 Richard Termine. Photos are credited on the pages on which they appear.

Photos from the Dieterle/Reinhardt 1935 production, Jiri Trnka's 1961 production, Michael Hoffman's 1999 production, and from the film of George Balanchine's 1962 ballet are courtesy of Douglas Lanier. Photos are credited on the pages on which they appear.

Postcard photos from the early 20th century are courtesy of Harry Rusche. Photos are credited on the pages on which they appear.

Photos from the Public Theater's 1961–1962 production directed by Joel Friedman, the 1974–75 production directed by Edward Berkeley, and the 1987–88 production directed by A. J. Antoon are copyright © 2005 George E. Joseph. Photos are credited on the pages on which they appear.

Photos from the 1999–2000 production at the Guthrie Theater directed by Joe Dowling are copyright © 2005 Michal Daniel. Photos are credited on the pages on which they appear.

Photos from the 1994 Royal Shakespeare Company production directed by Adrian Noble and of Kevin Kline and Michelle Pfeiffer in Michael

About the Contributors

TEXT EDITOR

Terri Bourus is an assistant professor of English at Indiana University Kokomo where she teaches Shakespeare and Renaissance Drama. She received her PhD in 2000 from Northern Illinois University. Her numerous publications include: "Working as a Director: An Interview with Aaron Posner" in *Shakespeare Bulletin*, 2003; "The First Quarto of Hamlet in Film: The Revenge-Tragedies of Nicol Williamson and Mel Gibson" in *EnterText*, 2001; *Shakespeare's 'Hamlet': Complete Study Edition*, edited by Sidney Lamb, 2000; and the upcoming text "Enter Hamlet [Reading on a book]: Shakespeare's Other Audience and the Publication of the Hamlet Quartos" in *Shakespeare's Book*, edited by Richard Wilson, 2006.

SERIES EDITORS

Marie Macaisa spent twenty years in her first career: high tech. She has a BS in computer science from the Massachusetts Institute of Technology and a MS in artificial intelligence from the University of Pennsylvania. She edited the first two books in the series, *Romeo and Juliet* and *Othello*, contributed the "Cast Speaks" essays, and is currently at work on the next set.

Dominique Raccah is the founder, president and publisher of Sourcebooks. Born in Paris, France, she has a bachelor's degree in psychology and a master's in quantitative psychology from the University of Illinois. She also serves as series editor of *Poetry Speaks* and *Poetry Speaks to Children*.

ADVISORY BOARD

David Bevington is the Phyllis Fay Horton Distinguished Service Professor in the Humanities at the University of Chicago. A renowned text scholar, he has edited several Shakespeare editions including the *Bantam Shakespeare* in individual paperback volumes, *The Complete Works of Shakespeare* (Longman, 2003), and *Troilus and Cressida* (Arden, 1998). He teaches courses in Shakespeare, renaissance drama, and medieval drama.

Peter Holland is the McMeel Family Chair in Shakespeare Studies at the University of Notre Dame. One of the central figures in performance-oriented Shakespeare criticism, he has also edited many Shakespeare plays, including *A Midsummer Night's Dream* for the Oxford Shakespeare series. He is also general editor of Shakespeare Survey and co-general editor (with Stanley Wells) of Oxford Shakespeare Topics. Currently he is completing a book, *Shakespeare on Film*, and editing *Coriolanus* for the Arden 3rd series.

Essayists

Thomas Garvey has been acting, directing, or writing about Shakespeare for over two decades. A graduate of the Massachusetts Institute of Technology, he studied acting and directing with the MIT Shakespeare Ensemble, where he played Hamlet, Jacques, Iago, and other roles, and directed *All's Well That Ends Well* and *Twelfth Night*. He has since directed and designed several other Shakespearean productions, as well as works by Chekhov, Ibsen, Sophocles, Beckett, Moliere, and Shaw. Mr. Garvey currently writes on theatre for the *Boston Globe* and other publications.

Douglas Lanier is an associate professor of English at the University of New Hampshire. He has written many essays on Shakespeare in popular culture, including "Shakescorp Noir" in *Shakespeare Quarterly* 53.2 (Summer 2002) and "Shakespeare on the Record" in *The Blackwell Companion to Shakespeare in Performance* (edited by Barbara Hodgdon and William Worthen, Blackwell, 2005). His book *Shakespeare and Modern Popular Culture* (Oxford University Press) was published in 2002. He is currently working on a book-length study of cultural stratification in early modern British theater.

Andrew Wade was head of voice for the Royal Shakespeare Company from 1990 to 2003 and voice assistant director from 1987 to 1990. During this time he worked on 170 productions and with more than 80 directors. Along with Cicely Berry, Andrew recorded *Working Shakespeare* and the DVD series *Voice and Shakespeare*, and he was the verse consultant for the movie *Shakespeare In Love*. In 2000, he won a Bronze Award from the New York International Radio Festival for the series *Lifespan*, which he co-directed and devised. He works widely teaching, lecturing and coaching throughout the world.